D1559504

THE PHENOMENOLOGICAL SENSE
OF JOHN DEWEY:
HABIT AND MEANING

The Phenomenological Sense
Of John Dewey:
HABIT AND MEANING

by

VICTOR KESTENBAUM

HUMANITIES PRESS

Atlantic Highlands, New Jersey

Copyright © 1977 by Humanities Press Inc.

No part of this book may be reproduced in any form without permission from the publisher, except for the quotation of brief passages in criticism.

Library of Congress Cataloging in Publication Data

Kestenbaum, Victor.
    The phenomenological sense of John Dewey:
    Habit and Meaning
    Bibliography: p.
  1. Dewey, John, 1859-1952. 2. Habit. 3. Meaning (Philosophy)
4. Phenomenology. I. Title.
B945.D44K47   191   76-41203
  ISBN 0-391-00668-1

Printed in the United States of America

PREFACE

In this study I have attempted to clarify and expand Dewey's concept of habit from an existential phenomenological perspective. The study reveals that Dewey's notion of habit is a theory of pre-objective, lived meaning, i.e., meaning which forms the context or field for the positing of distinct ideas or texts of reflective consciousness. By displaying the pre-objective intentionality of habitual lived meaning, the study establishes the phenomenological sense of Dewey, providing a basis for a more balanced and comprehensive view of his work. Dewey's logical theory and epistemology, his ethics and educational theory, are grounded in a theory of pre-reflective, habitual meaning. In recovering this phenomenological sense of Dewey's philosophy, I think we come closer to recovering its depth, subtlety, and power.

The study, in effect, exhibits the contours of one version of a genetic phenomenology. It elucidates the role of habitual, lived meanings in the genesis and functioning of reflective, predicative consciousness. A genetic phenomenology of this sort provides a philosophical context for understanding the development of individual and social meanings, and reflects the fundamental sense in which it may be said that habits are our inherence in time.

This work has profited from the criticisms and suggestions of James E. Wheeler, Bruce Wilshire, and J. J. Chambliss. Their understanding and appreciation of the diverse ways in which philosophy means, has deepened and refined my insights into the ambiguous ways in which philosophy educates.

My mother and father, Sarah and Louis Kestenbaum, are very much a part of the history of this work. My father did not live to see his son's efforts appear as a book, but his wisdom abides. From my wife, Eileen, and my daughter, Susan, I have learned a deeper meaning of many of the ideas considered in this study. To them, with love, I dedicate it.

Wellesley Hills, Ma.
April 14, 1976

CONTENTS

INTRODUCTION

Toward the end of the first chapter of *Experience and Nature,* Dewey comments that "the value of experience for the philosopher is that it serves as a constant reminder of something which is neither exclusive and isolated subject or object, matter or mind, nor yet one plus the other."[1] For his entire philosophic career, Dewey in one way or another was brought back to this realization that subject and object, self and world, cannot be specified independently of each other. His conception of organic interaction, and his later conception of transaction, were attempts to capture the reciprocal implication of self and world in every experienced situation. To Dewey, the experiencing-experienced interaction or transaction was a single structure, not two separate, discrete structures which somehow causally "act" upon one another.

Implicit in Dewey's notions of interaction and transaction is a well-developed conception of intentionality. According to this fundamental concept of phenomenology:

> Consciousness is not first something in itself and then enters also into relationship to something else. The relationship to the other enters into the very essence of the conscious act. Thus, it follows that consciousness is codetermined by the term to which it is related.[2]

The reciprocity of experiencing-experienced, intentional act-intentional object, is basic to Dewey's philosophy of experience. Schrag says "the question about intentionality is at bottom a question about meaning,"[3] and Dewey's inquiry into the meaning of experience serves his major purpose of better understanding the questions and problems involved in the experience of meanings.

---

[1]*Experience and Nature* (Chicago: Open Court Publishing Company, 1925), p. 28.

[2]Remy C. Kwant, *The Phenomenological Philosophy of Merleau-Ponty* (Pittsburg: Duquesne University Press, 1963), p. 154.

[3]Calvin O. Schrag, *Experience and Being: Prolegomena to a Future Ontology* (Evanston, Ill.: Northwestern University Press, 1969), p. 82.

Fundamental to Dewey's entire philosophy is his belief that "meaning is wider in scope as well as more precious in value than is truth, and philosophy is occupied with meaning rather than with truth."[4] Meaning is central not only to philosophy, for according to Dewey, "the characteristic human need is for possession and appreciation of the meaning of things."[5] Dewey's metaphysical interests in connection with the intentionality of human experience never strayed very far from his engrossing concern with the questions related to the experience of meanings. There is no question of primacy here, i.e., Dewey was not more interested in meaning than in say, ethics or logic or knowledge. The question of meaning did seem to Dewey, however, to insinuate itself into every facet of the affairs of man. The development, learning, sharing, and experiencing of meanings were central to Dewey's philosophy, for these activities gave content and purpose to any inquiry into questions such as the "meaning" of experience.

Some emphasis must be placed on the phrase, "the experience of meanings," because too often Dewey's concern with meaning is discussed from the fairly narrow perspective of linguistic meaning and its relationship to knowledge claims and truth claims. Dewey certainly was interested in this sense of meaning as shown in his *Essays in Experimental Logic,* and *Logic: The Theory of Inquiry.* Yet, even in these works it is always clear that Dewey is thinking within a broader context than linguistic meaning. Meanings are experienced by the human organism; they are "had" by the subject. It is a fundamental postulate of Dewey's theory of experience and theory of meaning that meanings must be "had" before they can be "known." Every aspect of Dewey's philosophy—epistemology, metaphysics, philosophy of education, ethics, political theory, and aesthetics—all are grounded in and reflect this conviction: "*being* and *having* things in ways other than knowing them, in ways never identical with knowing them, exist, and are preconditions of reflection and knowledge."[6]

Such "had" or "lived" meanings do not displace the importance of "known" meanings in human experience. Dewey's ontology of sense

---

[4]"Philosophy and Civilization," *Philosophy and Civilization* (New York: Minton, Balch & Company, 1931), p. 4.

[5]*Experience and Nature* (2nd ed.; Illinois: Open Court Publishing Company, 1929), p. 294.

[6]*Experience and Nature,* 1st ed., pp. 18-19.

is, however, an alternative to what he calls the "intellectualist fallacy" —the equation of the real and the known. The lived world of our doings and affections is not, Dewey believes, "in its primary phases a world that is known, a world that is understood, and is intellectually coherent and secure."[7] For Dewey, it was a "Copernican Revolution" that "we do not have to go to knowledge to obtain an exclusive hold on reality."[8] Immediately lived meanings disclose the world and order reality: that scientific method and knowledge have no monopoly on sensibility or intelligibility is a principle of Dewey's philosophy of experience which seems to have been almost willfully ignored by his admirers and critics.

The basis of Dewey's notion of meanings which are "had" or "lived" is his conception of habit. In *Human Nature and Conduct* he says that

> the word habit may seem twisted somewhat from its customary use when employed as we have been using it. But we need a word to express that kind of human activity which is influenced by prior activity and in that sense acquired; which contains within itself a certain ordering or systematization of minor elements of action; which is projective, dynamic in quality, ready for overt manifestation; and which is operative in some subdued form even when not obviously dominating activity.[9]

Habits are what Dewey variously calls "accepted meanings," "funded meanings," "acquired meanings," and "organic meanings." These habit-meanings or habitual meanings are the motivators of conscious behavior; furthermore, they are the basis of the unity of the organism. Perhaps even more fundamentally, however, the very intentional reciprocity of self and world is founded upon habits since, according to Dewey, "they constitute the self."[10] Habits reflect and record the outcomes of the individual's experiences; they provide the resources, in the form of taken for granted meanings, for his future experiences. Thus, in order to fully understand the organism's intentional relation-

---

[7]*The Quest for Certainty: A Study of the Relation of Knowledge and Action* (New York: Minton, Balch and Company, 1929), p. 295
[8]*Ibid.*
[9](New York: Modern Library, 1922), pp. 40-41. (Hereafter referred to as *Human Nature.*)
[10]*Ibid.*, p. 25.

ship to the environment, it is necessary to properly appreciate the intentionality of habit.

Habits are not, in Dewey's formulation, experienced by the organism as cognitive or even conscious phenomena. Habits operate on a level of experience which precedes any sort of deliberate, critical positing of distinct *objects* of reflection or consciousness. In this sense, then, habits are pre-objective, i.e., they are prior to any deliberate positing or specification of objects of knowledge or awareness. According to Dewey, man is a sense-giving being on a level of experience which is pre-reflective and pre-conscious, i.e., on that level of experience which is man's original access or opening to the world.

The presence of habitual meanings in ordinary experience is pervasive and extensive. The driver of an automobile takes advantage of perceptual, motor, and cognitive meanings which are embodied in its organism as pre-reflective, pre-conscious habits. A child's or adult's engrossment in a game reflects the silent (though powerful) workings of pre-critical, pre-objective habit. Being in a strange or unfamiliar situation confounds and confuses: the taken-for-granted meanings of embodied habit are inadequate for "making sense" of the situation. The perceptual habits of the Westerner are such that Oriental music strikes him as oddly lacking in melody or rhythm. An experienced sailor possesses a field of habitual meanings enabling him to simultaneously pilot his craft, compensate for a change in wind velocity, and note the roll of a sail.

In the realm of less ordinary or mundane experience, the scientist relies upon pre-reflective habits, for example, habits of observation, selection, reflection, and interpretation. Paradigms, in Thomas Kuhn's sense,[11] exert their influence by forming and sustaining individual and collective habits: pre-reflective, lived meanings which are the record of previously accumulated experience. To be influenced and guided by a paradigm is less a matter of knowing it as a series of rules or propositions, but rather is more a case of living it as an atmosphere of tacit meaning founded on the world-disclosing possibilities of pre-objective habit. In Dewey's terms, paradigms are had or lived before they are known—to have a paradigm is to have a habit.

In all these instances, ordinary and scientific, there are meanings

11*The Structure of Scientific Revolutions,* 2nd ed. (Chicago: University of Chicago Press, 1970).

present but not visible in the experienced situation, meanings which are not merely present in some passive sense, but which, in interaction with the world or environment, are constitutive of the situation as it is experienced or had by the organism. For Dewey, experience of any kind reveals the world-founding possibilities of habit, i.e., the creative, constitutive power of habitual meanings to pre-reflectively and pre-consciously establish self and world as moments of a single rhythm.

The purpose of the present study is to elucidate Dewey's notion of habit from the standpoint of pre-objective intentionality. There is no intention in the study to make a case that Dewey was a "proto-phenomenologist" or that certain features of his philosophy of experience "anticipate" concerns of modern phenomenology. The only possible value to be derived from an attempt to interpret Dewey from a phenomenological orientation, is to draw closer attention to aspects and features of his philosophy which either have been neglected (to the detriment of an appreciation of the power and subtlety of Dewey's philosophy of experience), or commonly misunderstood. This benefit can be achieved without claiming that Dewey was a phenomenologist. Too much of Dewey's meaning has been overlooked or misinterpreted as a result of the ascription of one label after another to his philosophy. Certainly, to burden Dewey's philosophy with one more label cannot possibly serve any reasonable end.

The reason for elucidating Dewey's notion of habit from the standpoint of pre-objective intentionality, is that such a strategy helps to make the greatest sense out of this concept. The dramatic, creative meaning of habit, the human meaning of habit, simply cannot be grasped until its sense-producing character is traced to its pre-reflective, pre-predicative foundation. Husserl was one of the first to undertake this archaeology. Early in *Experience and Judgment,* he frames his discussion of pre-predicative experience, the life-world, in terms of habit:

> Though we have already acquired a concept of experience as objective self-evidence of individual objects, such experience is still multiform in itself, even if all the idealizations which overlie its originality have been dismantled. Our life-world in its originality, which can be brought to light only by the destruction of those layers of sense, is not only, as has already been mentioned, a world of logical operations, not only the realm of the pregivenness of objects as possible judicative substrates,

as possible themes of cognitive activity, but it is also the world of experience in the wholly concrete sense which is commonly tied in with the word "experience." And this commonplace sense is in no way related purely and simply to cognitive behavior; taken in its greatest generality, it is related, rather, to a habituality [*Habitualität*] which lends to him who is provided with it, to him who is "experienced," assurance in decision and action in the situations of life—whether these situations are definitely limited or are understood in general as comprising an attitude toward life on the whole—just as, on the other hand, by this expression we are also concerned with the individual steps of the "experience" by which this habituality is acquired. Thus this commonplace, familiar, and concrete sense of the word "experience" points much more to a mode of behavior which is practically active and evaluative than specifically to one that is cognitive and judicative.[12]

Later, in Section 25, "The precipitate of explication *in habitus.* The act of impressing something upon oneself," Husserl expands his treatment of habit as the organic embodiment and retention of lived experience: a meaning constituted in lived experience and retained by the organism is, Husserl says, a *"possession in the form of a habitus."*[13]

This grounding of the lived in the habitual does not receive detailed elaboration by Husserl, hence, it would be incautious to attribute an importance to habit which it simply may not have in the general effort of his phenomenology. Yet, Husserl's identification of "the Ego as substrate of habitualities"[14] in the *Cartesian Meditations;* his belief that "with the doctrine of the Ego as pole of his acts and substrate of habitualities, we have already touched on the *problems of phenomenological genesis* and done so at a significant point,"[15] these seem to suggest that habit is closer to being a major (though unexplicated) concept in Husserl's phenomenology rather than a minor one.

It is Merleau-Ponty, then, who most systematically establishes the pre-objective intentionality of habitual meaning as the foundation of

[12]*Experience and Judgment: Investigations in a Genealogy of Logic,* trans. by James S. Churchill and Karl Ameriks (Evanston: Northwestern University Press, 1973), p. 52.
[13]*Ibid.,* p. 122.
[14]*Cartesian Meditations*: *An Introduction to Phenomenology,* trans. by Dorion Cairns (The Hague: Martinus Nijhoff 1960), p. 66.
[15]*Ibid.,* p. 69.

a genetic and existential phenomenology. Remarkably, Merleau-Ponty has suffered the same fate as Dewey: the role of the habitual in his philosophy has been given inadequate attention by both his admirers and detractors. Although a great deal is made of his notion of the "corps propre," the "body-subject," and "incarnated intentionality," there is little recognition of the fact that whenever Merleau-Ponty spoke of the intentionality of the body, he was referring to the *habitual body*. It was clear to Merleau-Ponty, if not to his critics, that man's being-in-the-world is by nature an habitual-being-in-the-world.[16]

The point at which Dewey and Merleau-Ponty are philosophically the closest, is in their common understanding that habit is the organic structure which grounds the human pole of pre-objective intentionality. It would be a mistake, however, to fail to recognize the similarity of their views with respect to experience. Thus, Merleau-Ponty writes:

> The physicist's atoms will always appear more real than the historical and qualitative face of the world, the physico-chemical processes more real than the organic forms, the psychological atoms of empiricism more real than perceived phenomena, the intellectual atoms represented by the "significations" of the Vienna Circle more real than consciousness, as long as the attempt is made to build up the shape of the world (life, perception, mind) instead of recognizing, as the source which stares us in the face and as the ultimate court of appeal in our knowledge of these things, our *experience* of them.[17]

In addition to sharing a common understanding of what may be termed the "primacy of experience," Dewey and Merleau-Ponty were united in their opposition to (1) dualisms of any kind, (2) that sort of intellectualism which would reduce all experience to experience of knowing, and (3) scientism. The similarity of Dewey and Merleau-Ponty does not rest merely upon what they were opposed to. The alternatives they offered in place of what they were opposed to also share a striking similarity. It is beyond the scope of this Introduction, and not necessary for the purposes of this study, to establish this similarity of

---

[16]Maurice Merleau-Ponty, *Phenomenology of Perception*, trans. by Colin Smith (New York: Humanities Press, 1962), p. 441. (Hereafter referred to as *Phenomenology*.)

[17]*Ibid.*, p. 23.

Dewey's and Merleau-Ponty's philosophical positions. Merleau-Ponty's work on the pre-objective intentionality of habit provides a suitable context for elucidating Dewey's conception of habit. Naturally, Merleau-Ponty's phenomenology of habitual, pre-reflective meaning will itself come into sharper focus in functioning as a context for treating Dewey, but this is a secondary consequence of the study, not its primary intention.

It will not be, then, the aim of this study to explicitly compare Dewey and Merleau-Ponty on the notion of habit. Although such a comparison is implicit in the study, its major purpose is to uncover (and in a very definite sense, recover) the pre-objective intentionality *always* implicit and sometimes explicit in Dewey's use of habit. The pre-objective intentionality of habit has been hidden and obscured by generations of readers who simply have been unable to recognize, much less understand, the extraordinarily subtle and complex sense in which Dewey conceived of habit. In order to realize the purpose of this study, it is necessary to go beyond the banality typical of most discussions of his work, and especially discussions, what there are of them, of his conception of habit.

Dewey's use of habit as a philosophical category spanned at least sixty-five years. One possible method of elucidating his notion of habit would be to follow its historical development from his Hegelian "period" of the 1880's to the last years of his life. Such a method has obvious values and advantages, not the least of which is that it is consistent with Dewey's emphasis on respecting the historical character of all experience. Eventually, such a study will be necessary if Dewey's conception of habit is to be fully uncovered and brought to light.

This historical method will not be employed in the present study, however. In order to establish at least the minimal plausibility that Dewey's theory of habit is analyzable in terms of pre-objective intentionality, it is necessary to see *how it functions* in a particular philosophical discussion, i.e., it is necessary to *describe* the work it does in furthering a particular philosophical argument. Although "necessary" is probably too strong a word here, it does seems that hasty and misleading generalizations and distinctions can be avoided very effectively when description of a phenomenon in a specified context precedes analysis.

Dewey's *Art as Experience* offers just such a context. Because aesthetic experience was to Dewey an intensification[18] and purification of ordinary experience, the functioning of habit during such experience offers an opportunity to view it when it functions at its most delicate and profound best. In an aesthetic experience, the traits of habit become manifest and magnified; its pre-objective intentionality can be seen with clear definition and in high relief against the background of non-aesthetic experience.

It is not usually appreciated to just what extent Dewey considered aesthetic experience as a realization of the possibilities of ordinary, common, non-aesthetic experience. Even less is it appreciated to just what extent Dewey considered a philosopher's account of aesthetic experience to be the most basic test of the soundness of his philosophy. Dewey asserts that for any philosopher, aesthetic experience

> is a test of the capacity of the system he puts forth to grasp the nature of experience itself. There is no test that so surely reveals the one-sidedness of a philosophy as its treatment of art and esthetic experience.[19]

If habits are the basis of the pre-objective intentionality of experience, then one could not do better than turn to aesthetic experience for elucidation of this fact, for it was Dewey's strongly held belief that "to esthetic experience . . . the philosopher must go to understand what experience is."[20]

The present study is, then, an interpretation, an elucidation, of *Art as Experience* from the standpoint of the pre-objective intentionality of habit. Merleau-Ponty's phenomenology of the habitual body will provide a convenient context from which to view the character of Dewey's conception of the pre-objective intentionality of habit. A context is by nature taken for granted, i.e., it does not enter into a discussion as an object of explicit conscious concern or treatment. This is the case with

---

[18]It will be seen that Dewey's constant reminder that aesthetic experience "intensifies" the qualities and conditions of ordinary experience, is enormously important in understanding the intentionality of habit. The word "intense" is derived from the Latin *intensus,* pp. of *intendere,* meaning to stretch out for, aim at, and it is from this Latin verb that the English "intend" is derived. The study will reveal in what sense Dewey took aesthetic experience to be an intensification of the intentionality of habit.

[19]*Art as Experience* (New York: Minton, Balch and Company, 1934), p. 274.

[20]*Ibid.*

the context provided by Merleau-Ponty's phenomenology of the habitual body. It is always present, but not visibly so. It acts as a sort of gauge whereby the character and movement of Dewey's thought can be seen with greater clarity and, presumably, increased understanding.

The study is clearly more descriptive than analytical. Every attempt has been made to let Dewey speak for himself, i.e., to follow the course of his argument and observe how habit functions in its development without introducing concepts and considerations which are not unambiguously implied by the progress of his own thought. At the conclusion of his essay on "The Postulate of Immediate Empiricism," Dewey says that the philosophical method suggested by his postulate "is not spectacular; it permits of no offhand demonstrations of God, freedom, immortality, nor of the exclusive reality of matter, or ideas, or consciousness, etc."[21] Much the same can be said about the method employed in this study. It will not allow any "offhand demonstrations" that Dewey was working certain phenomenological themes, nor that his philosophy of experience in some ways anticipates recent studies by certain existential phenomenologists. Yet, by seeing Dewey's "phenomenological sense" revealed and magnified in *Art as Experience,* the reader will be enabled to assess the significance of this "sense" with respect to its role in Dewey's entire philosophy, as well as its relevance to other areas of human inquiry.

---

[21]*The Influence of Darwin on Philosophy* (Bloomington: Indiana University Press, 1910), p. 239. (Hereafter referred to as "Immediate Empiricism.")

CHAPTER 1

THE LIVE CREATURE

Aesthetic experience, according to Dewey, is not only continuous with ordinary experience; it is also an intensification of the qualities and conditions of ordinary experience. In order to support his claim that aesthetic experience is an intense expression of the "full meaning of ordinary experience," Dewey briefly discusses what he takes to be the "conditions and factors that make an ordinary experience complete."[1] His discussion of these conditions is highly schematic, undoubtedly because he had devoted considerable attention to interaction and continuity in previous works. In addition, "The Live Creature" is the first chapter of *Art as Experience,* and Dewey very likely was content merely to outline those conditions which were to receive more extensive treatment in the course of the work. However, an analysis and expansion of Dewey's discussion of interaction and continuity of experiences will serve to introduce the role of habit in ordinary experience, as well as aesthetic experience.

The first condition, or "great consideration" as Dewey calls it, is that "life goes on in an environment; not merely *in* it but because of it, through interaction with it."[2] The environment is the "natural medium" which poses threats and dangers to the well-being of the live creature. It also provides the means whereby the needs of the live creature are satisfied. Need satisfaction in man is not, however, "mere return to a prior state" because the resistance of the environment makes possible "a more extensive balance of the energies of the organism with those of the conditions under which it lives."[3] Resistance, opposition, and conflict are not unfortunate circumstances of life. On the contrary, tension is necessary for the intensification of present powers and capacities. Without such expansion and intensification of present abil-

---

[1]*Art as Experience*, p. 12.
[2]*Ibid.*, p. 13.
[3]*Ibid.*, p. 14.

11

ities, the environment remains diminished in scope and impoverished in quality, thus limiting or restricting the potential of the environment in eliciting more complex behavior and experience. The "circularity" of such a conception of interaction was not regretted by Dewey. He considered it to be a basic feature of all experience, an expression of the constant rhythm of loss and recovery of integration which marks the life of the live creature in interaction with its environment.

The equilibrium, then, which follows the loss of integration with environment is not the outcome of a mechanical process. "Dynamic" might be used to describe the nature of this recovery of integration, but its overuse has seriously affected its descriptive and explanatory utility. Perhaps the meanings associated with the word "dramatic" serve to emphasize in what sense the loss and recovery of integration involves a continuously developing situation marked by purpose and direction, yet one still possessing a certain degree of ambiguity or indeterminateness with respect to the outcome or consummation. Such dramatic integration or equilibrium is the basis of form. Dewey writes: "Form is arrived at whenever a stable, even though moving, equilibrium is reached."[4] In the same sense that the order of a dramatic situation develops out of the energies that are internal to it, form or order "is not imposed from without but is made out of the relations of harmonious interactions that energies bear to one another."[5] Because the artist is uniquely concerned with experience that is integrated, unified, and whole, he does not, Dewey says, "shun moments of resistance and tension." Aesthetic experience, then, is an intensification of the basic rhythm of interaction between the live creature and environment. On the level of ordinary experience this interaction already possesses dramatic qualities. Aesthetic experience is an intensification of the dramatic qualities of ordinary, concrete experience.

Dewey himself offers evidence that interaction and integration bear more than a superficial resemblance to drama. He writes:

> Contrast of lack and fullness, of struggle and achievement, of adjustment after consummated irregularity, form the drama in which action, feeling, and meaning are one. The outcome is balance and counterbalance. These are not static nor me-

———————
[4]Ibid.
[5]Ibid.

chanical. They express power that is intense because measured through overcoming resistance. Environing objects avail and counteravail.[6]

Dewey at this point is anticipating his later argument: the drama of interaction is only potentially capable of that kind of unity wherein "action, feeling, and meaning are one." Nevertheless, Dewey's intention is clear. Through interaction, a drama is enacted wherein the functioning structures of the human organism are reorganized or reconstructed in such a manner that their operation is rendered more integrated or harmonious. It is not the state of achieved harmony which Dewey wishes to celebrate. Instead, "the moment of passage from disturbance into harmony is that of intensest life."[7] The state of harmony is significant, aesthetically or otherwise, when it is the consummation of a process born out of tension and resistance.

Dewey is careful to emphasize that "inner harmony" is not the work of some subjective, self-contained force or power. The harmony he speaks of is "attained only when, by some means, terms are made with the environment," and for this reason, when inner harmony "occurs on any other than an 'objective' basis, it is illusory—in extreme cases to the point of insanity." Dewey does not pursue the subjective-objective problem at this point, but instead chooses to take his discussion of harmony as an opportunity to move from the first condition of complete experiences, that of interaction, to his second condition, the continuity of experiences. Dewey's treatment of this second condition is brief, in fact, it is actually only one paragraph. Nevertheless, it was undoubtedly clear to Dewey that the significance of interaction would be seriously limited if the results of interaction were not somehow retained and funded by the human organism. Dewey's transition from the condition of interaction to that of continuity is effected by his statement that through dramatic interaction and integration "there abides the deep-seated memory of an underlying harmony, the sense of which haunts life like the sense of being founded on a rock."[8]

The harmony and unity of organism-environment is possible Dewey says, "only when the past ceases to trouble and anticipations of

---

[6]*Ibid.*, p. 16.
[7]*Ibid.*, p. 17.
[8]*Ibid.*

the future are not perturbing." Unlike much of ordinary experience where past, present, and future exist in a fragmented and disjointed manner, "in life that is truly life, everything overlaps and merges." Complete experience is temporally unified and integrated, in addition to it being a unification of organism and environment. Complete experience is an intensification of the field of time; the present is a dramatic overture to the future and fulfillment of the past. In Dewey's words: "Art celebrates with peculiar intensity the moments in which the past re-enforces the present and in which the future is a quickening of what now is."[9]

Interaction and continuity of experience constitute, as Dewey says in *Experience and Education,* the longitudinal and lateral aspects of ordinary and aesthetic experience. Different interactions or situations succeed one another, "but because of the principle of continuity something is carried over from the earlier to the later ones."[10] Unity of experience, completeness of experience, demand a unity of time and a unity of interaction. Dewey sees such unity of experience exemplified in the "activities of the fox, the dog, and the thrush." He writes:

> The live animal is fully present, all there, in all of its actions: in its wary glances, its sharp sniffings, its abrupt cocking of ears. All senses are equally on the *qui vive.* As you watch, you see motion merging into sense and sense into motion—constituting that animal grace so hard for man to rival. What the live creature retains from the past and what it expects from the future operate as directions in the present.[11]

Dewey finds the "sources of esthetic experience" in "animal life below the human scale" because the unity and integration of the live animal itself, and the unity and integration of the live animal and environment, exemplify the conditions which aesthetic experience develops and intensifies.

To Dewey, the savage embodied in pure form, if not sophisticated or complex form, the qualities and conditions of dramatic life, life which is "fully alive." According to Dewey, the savage

is as active through his whole being when he looks and listens

---

[9]*Ibid.,* p. 18.
[10]*Experience and Education* (New York: Macmillan Company, 1938), p. 44.
[11]*Art as Experience,* p. 19.

as when he stalks his quarry or stealthily retreats from a foe. His senses are sentinels of immediate thought and outposts of action, and not, as they so often are with us, mere pathways along which material is gathered to be stored away for a delayed and remote possibility.[12]

It is clear that Dewey attributes great importance to the fact that the savage is alive with his "whole being." It is not entirely clear, however, what he in fact means by "whole being." Apparently, Dewey wants to say that the savage, in his interactions with the environment, is "whole" in the sense that action, feeling, and meaning are unified or integrated. Furthermore, the savage is "whole" in the sense that the present is organically continuous with the past and future. There is, however, a certain abstractness in Dewey's reference to the savage's "whole being," as indeed there is in his general discussion of interaction and continuity. How is the past present? How and what does the human organism contribute to an interaction? These questions are, of course, the subject of much of Dewey's writing. However, it is in a very early essay, "Interpretation of the Savage Mind,"[13] where he gives one of his most powerful accounts of these problems, primarily because in it he gives profound consideration to what may be called the drama of habit.

Dewey's intention in this essay is to provide a "proper method of interpretation," whereby what he calls the "patterns," "forms," or "schema" of the savage mind may be subject to systematic investigation. He identifies occupations as the primary source of the structures of mind. "Occupations determine the fundamental modes of activity, and hence control the formation and use of habits."[14] There can be little doubt that the patterns, types, forms, and structures to which Dewey refers, are embodied in the organism as habits. At the conclusion of the essay he says:

> Let me point out that the adjustment of habits to ends, through the medium of a problematic, doubtful, precarious situation, is the structural form upon which present intelligence and emotion are built. It remains the ground-pattern.[15]

---

[12]*Ibid.*
[13]*Philosophy and Civilization* (New York: Minton, Balch & Company, 1931). (Hereafter referred to as "Savage Mind.")
[14]*Ibid.*, p. 175.
[15]*Ibid.*, p. 187.

What Dewey wishes to do is to show that the primary occupation of a social group—his example is hunting—develops a "psychic pattern," a unique configuration of habits which informs and qualifies every activity of the group—art, war, marriage, religion, and so on. Dewey's argument is that if such psychic patterns and habits can be shown to exert a differential controlling influence, i.e., if there can be shown to be a psychic pattern typical of the hunting life, a pattern typical of the farming life, the military life, and so on, then there will be "an important method for the interpretation of social institutions and cultural resources—a psychological method for sociology."[16]

In order to illustrate the use of such an interpretive method, and furthermore, to reveal how "psychic patterns" and "psychic habits" are formed and organized, Dewey discusses the hunting life of the Australian aborigines. According to Dewey, the Australian's "psychic pattern" is one of "immediacy of interest, attention and deed."[17] The key word here, of course, is "immediacy," and in order to emphasize its meaning with respect to the hunter, Dewey first describes the temporal world of the farming life. Dewey writes:

> The gathering and saving of seed, preparing the ground, sowing, tending, weeding, care of cattle, making of improvements, continued observation of times and seasons, engage thought and direct action. In a word, in all post-hunting situations the end is mentally apprehended and appreciated not as food satisfaction, but as a continuously ordered series of activities and of objective contents pertaining to them. And hence the direct and personal display of energy, personal putting forth of effort, personal acquisition and use of skill are not conceived or felt as immediate parts of the food process.[18]

In striking contrast to this world of the farmer, the world of the hunter is characterized by a pervasive sense of immediacy. As Dewey says: "There are no intermediate appliances, no adjustment of means to remote ends, no postponements of satisfaction, no transfer of interest and attention over to a complex system of acts and objects."[19] Past and future are not sharply marked off from each other since they "meet

---

[16]*Ibid.*, p. 196.
[17]*Ibid.*, p. 178.
[18]*Ibid.*
[19]*Ibid.*

and are lost in the stress of the present problem." Neither tools, weapons, or the land itself are experienced as "means" to some remote end; hence, they are not matters of objective regard or analysis, but instead are lived as "fused" portions of life.

Dewey is saying, then, that the occupation of hunting develops or establishes a peculiar psychic pattern or structure which is embodied in the organic body as a particular configuration of certain kinds of habits. These habits motivate behavior and experience in such a manner that most interactions of the hunter come to be guided and influenced by the same sense of immediacy that the occupation of hunting typifies. "Immediacy of interest, attention and deed" become pervasive qualities of the entire world of the hunter. Because the habits of the hunter do not allow for a sense of the past or future, but only a profound sense of the immediate present, he values only those objects and conditions which contribute to an intensification or dramatization of the immediate display of intellectual and practical abilities. "Consciousness, even if superficial, is maintained at a higher intensity."[20] Through his habits of mind and body, the Australian hunter lives in a world which is dramatic in a most pregnant sense of the word. The habits of the hunter require an environment, a world, wherein the drama of the hunt is enacted in all situations and interactions. The habits formed in the activity of hunting come to constitute what Merleau-Ponty calls an "inner diaphragm":

> Prior to stimuli and sensory contents, we must recognize a kind of inner diaphragm which determines, infinitely more than they do, what our reflexes and perceptions will be able to aim at in the world, the area of our possible operations, the scope of our life.[21]

Thus, the being-in-the-world of the Australian hunter is fundamentally dramatic; the structures or forms of his body-mind, as embodied in organic habits, carve out a world wherein the suspense and tension of drama are normative and regulative.

In order to show how "deeply embedded" the hunting pattern or schema is in the Australian aborigines, Dewey proceeds to examine various aspects of the life of the Australian. His first example is art.

---

[20]*Ibid.,* p. 179.
[21]*Phenomenology,* p. 79.

He says that "the art of the Australian is not constructive, not architectonic, not graphic, but dramatic and mimetic." Painting, dances, and ceremonies are all dramatic representations and serve to "revive the feelings appropriate to the immediate conflict-situations."[22]

Turning next to religion, Dewey considers totemism as a particularly powerful expression of the hunting pattern or schema. In his discussion of totemism, Dewey provides a profound insight into the nature of habit. He says: "Hunter and hunted are the factors of a single tension; the mental situation cannot be defined except in terms of both."[23] Dewey is here establishing the intentional nature of habit. The habits of the hunter solicit certain kinds of responses from the environment. Similarly, the environment solicits certain responses from the hunter, responses mediated by the "inner diaphragm" of the hunter —his embodied habits. As will be seen later, in claiming that aesthetic experience is an intensification of the conditions of ordinary experience, Dewey is in effect claiming that aesthetic experience is a dramatization of the intentional nature of consciousness. It is sufficient to note here that the mutual or reciprocal implication of hunter and hunted in a "single tension" is merely another way of stating Merleau-Ponty's contention that

> situation and reaction are linked internally by their common participation in a structure in which the mode of activity proper to the organism is expressed. Hence they cannot be placed one after the other as cause and effect: they are two moments of a circular process.[24]

Hunter and hunted are two moments in a "single tension."

Dewey concludes his "interpretation of the savage mind" by discussing death, sickness, marriage, and sex. It is unnecessary to trace in full his account of how these phenomena make sense in terms of the hunting pattern or schema. Dewey succeeds in showing that in all of his life experiences, the Australian hunter is guided by habits which reflect the drama of the hunt. He affirms that the attention of the Australians "is mobile and fluid as is their life; they are eager to the point

22"Savage Mind," p. 183.
23Ibid., p. 184.
24The Structure of Behavior, trans. by Alden L. Fisher (Boston: Beacon Press, 1963), p. 130.

of greed for anything which will fit into their dramatic situations so as to intensify skill and increase emotion."[25] Being-in-the-world is a matter of being-in-situations; the being-in-the-world of the Australian hunter is dramatic in the basic sense of being a celebration of tensed situations. However, the situations which make up the world of the hunter, situations which so completely implicate both hunter and hunted that they are a "single tension," could not possibly exist if the hunter was not a live creature possessed of certain habits. The possibility of being in a situation rests upon the possibility of having habits.

More than any other attribute of man, habit expresses the fundamental nature of being-in-the-world. Twenty years after the publication of his essay on the savage, Dewey asserted that "man is a creature of habit, not of reason nor yet of instinct."[26] Yet, already in 1902, forty-three years before Merleau-Ponty's discovery of the same fact, Dewey recognized that man is a being-in-the-world by virtue of his habits; man fundamentally is an habitual-being-in-the-world.

Having considered the drama of habit in the life of the savage hunter, it is somewhat clearer what Dewey is referring to when he speaks of the savage's "whole being" at the end of "The Live Creature." The live creature—animal, savage, man—is a creature of habit; the "whole being" of the savage is his being as embodied in the habits of body-mind. In the thirty-two year interval separating "Interpretation of the Savage Mind" and *Art as Experience,* Dewey of course had refined and expanded his notion of habit to the point where habit unambiguously became the basis of the unity of the organism. Dewey says:

> All habits are demands for certain kinds of activity; and they constitute the self. In any intelligible sense of the word will, they *are* will. They form our effective desires and they furnish us with our working capacities.[27]

The "working capacities" which Dewey attributes to the functioning of habits are remarkable not merely because of their number, but also because they express such basic and distinctive activities of being human. He says that "habits formed in process of exercising biological aptitudes

---

[25]"Savage Mind," p. 182.
[26]*Human Nature,* p. 125.
[27]*Ibid.,* p. 25.

are the sole agents of observation, recollection, foresight and judgment."[28] As if not satisfied that he has adequately conveyed the pervasive presence of habits in all human experience, Dewey continues, saying:

> Concrete habits do all the perceiving, recognizing, imagining, recalling, judging, conceiving and reasoning that is done. 'Consciousness,' whether as a stream or as special sensations and images, express functions of habits, phenomena of their formation, operation, their interruption and reorganization.[29]

To understand what Dewey means by claiming that the savage's "senses are sentinels of immediate thought and outposts of action," it must be born in mind that he has assumed that sense, thought, and action are a function of habit. Furthermore, Dewey's contention that the more numerous and flexible habits are, "the more refined is perception in its discrimination and the more delicate the presentation evoked by imagination,"[30] provides a clue to the meaning and significance of the concluding sentence of "The Live Creature," "delightful perception . . . is esthetic experience."

Early in the second chapter Dewey introduces the notion of "fusion" as part of his general discussion of the ontology of sense. He laments the fact that frequently senses do not fuse, making impossible a "deep realization of intrinsic meanings." This lack of unity or fusion of the senses results in a decreased "sense of the reality" of perceived objects. Seeing is not informed by the qualities of hearing; touch is lifeless and mechanical because not pregnant with the qualities of sight.

In contrast to such fragmentation of man's being, the savage is active through his "whole being"; his perceptual habits, motor habits, and whatever linguistic habits he may possess, operate in such a coordinated, organized manner that fusion does not seem too strong a word to describe the functioning of these habits. In referring to the fusion of the senses, Dewey means the interpenetration of habits of eye, ear, touch, smell, and taste. It quickly becomes clear, however, that Dewey is concerned not only with the habits of the senses, but rather all the habits of the live creature's body-mind. If the habits of the live

---

[28]*Ibid.*, p. 176.
[29]*Ibid.*, p. 177.
[30]*Ibid.*, pp. 175-76.

creature did not possess some degree of organization or structure, "conduct would lack unity being only a juxtaposition of disconnected reactions to separate situations."[31] Because "the senses are the organs through which the live creature participates directly in the ongoings of the world about him,"[32] perception is, so to speak, the point of contact between the world and all the acquired and funded meanings of the organism which are embodied in its organic habits, and which make it possible for the organism to be in the world and have a world.

It is perhaps somewhat clearer now why Dewey identified "delightful perception" with aesthetic experience at the conclusion of the first chapter, and why this identification is an assumption of the entire work. In sense or perceptual experience, the mutual implication or mutual reciprocity of self and world is most direct, immediate, and complete. Dewey writes: "Sense, as meaning so directly embdied in experience as to be its own illuminated meaning, is the only signification that expresses the function of sense organs when they are carried to full realization."[33] The interaction of organism and environment, or in Merleau-Ponty's terms, the dialectic of organic individual and milieu, is an affair, as Dewey says, of "doings and undergoings." Experience is, however, "a matter of *simultaneous* doings and sufferings."[34] The individual's habits solicit a certain range of responses from the world; they do something to or act upon the world by forming a situation. The world, however, is also active, and the habits of the organism must respond to the solicitation of the world as manifested in the particularity of an experienced situation. In perception, then, when it is not merely recognition, all the habits of the organism, all the "constituents of his being," are not only potentially active, but active in such a tensed yet ordered way, that such dramatic perceptual experience comes to constitute for Dewey the criterion distinguishing aesthetic from non-aesthetic experience.

It should be obvious that Dewey has purposefully blurred any distinction between perceptual meaning and cognitive or intellectual meaning. In perception, the habits of the organism may fuse or inter-

---

[31]*Ibid.*, p. 38.

[32]Dewey, *Art as Experience*, p. 22.

[33]*Ibid.*

[34]"The Need for a Recovery of Philosophy," in *John Dewey on Experience, Nature, and Freedom*, ed. by Richard J. Bernstein (New York: Liberal Arts Press, 1960), p. 26.

penetrate in such a fashion that the senses become, as with the savage, "sentinels of immediate thought and outposts of action." Unfortunately, however, the life of modern man is, according to Dewey, "stunted, aborted, slack, or heavy laden," and therefore aesthetic experience as "delightful perception" is commonly considered as somehow being quite different in kind from ordinary perception and experience. Dewey, of course, is in fundamental disagreement with such a point of view. Habits which in one context operate mechanically and without interpenetration, causing the fragmentation of the organism into realms of cognition, perception, action, and feeling, can become in another context the basis of that "delightful perception" which is aesthetic. Dewey says that "art is the living and concrete proof that man is capable of restoring consciously, and thus, on the plane of meaning, the union of sense, need, impulse and action characteristic of the live creature."[35]

Although Dewey is very concerned to establish the unity of the senses among themselves and with other aspects of the human organism, his main purpose in "The Live Creature and 'Ethereal Things' " is not to argue this point. His basic concern in this chapter is to show that "there is no limit to the capacity of immediate sensuous experience to absorb into itself meanings and values that in and of themselves— that is in the abstract—would be designated 'ideal' and 'spiritual.' "[36] One of the conditions necessary for such perceptual meanings is the fusion or interpenetration of perceptual, cognitive and motor habits. Perceptual meanings are continuous with other kinds of meanings and may embody other meanings because perceptual habits affect and are affected by other habits. The habits of an organism form a pattern, configuration, or structure wherein each habit contributes to the total configuration, and the configuration affects the functioning of any particular habit. Naturally, some configurations of habits show a greater degree of integration than other configurations. Dewey is very clear in connection with this point. He says that

> integration is an achievement rather than a datum. A weak, unstable, vacillating character is one in which different habits alternate with one another rather than embody one another. The strength, solidity of a habit is not its own possession but

---

[35]*Art as Experience*, p. 25.
[36]*Ibid.*, p. 29.

is due to reinforcement by the force of other habits which it absorbs into itself.[37]

Because of this integration of habits, "the sensible surface of things is never merely a surface."[38] The meanings embodied in perceptual habits, cognitive habits, and motor habits, endow the sensed surface with a "depth of meaning" which it would lack if perception were unaffected by the whole configuration of organic habits.

Throughout most of the chapter, Dewey makes isolated references to matters or events which are, as he says, "merely intellectual." Dewey makes explicit the thrust of these statements in concluding the second chapter with what might be called a "critique of reason." Using as a basis for his discussion Keats' letter describing Shakespeare as a man of enormous "negative capability," Dewey asserts that " 'reason' at its height cannot attain complete grasp and a self-contained assurance. It must fall back upon imagination—upon the embodiment of ideas in emotionally charged sense."[39] At first, it is not altogether clear what Dewey is intending by use of such phrases as "imaginative sentiments" and "imaginative intuitions." He has established, for his own purposes, the primacy of the senses and perception, but it is unclear how sense and imagination are related according to Dewey. This vagueness reveals itself to be more apparent than real, however, when Dewey's conception of imagination is made explicit. He says that "an imaginative experience is what happens when varied materials of sense quality, emotion, and meaning come together in a union that marks a new birth in the world."[40] Imagination is a particular manifestation of the comprehensive interpenetration of habits. "Imaginative sentiments" and "imaginative intuitions" are expressions of habits as they form and reform new structures or configurations. Such "sentiments" and "intuitions" reveal the actual and potential dramatic nature of habits as highly tensed, incomplete structures or configurations achieve greater integration and completeness. Because "man lives in a world of surmise, of mystery, of uncertainties,"[41] its drama can be only incompletely known and appreciated by reason alone. Reason itself must be nurtured by the drama

---

[37]*Human Nature,* p. 38.
[38]Dewey, *Art as Experience,* p. 29.
[39]*Ibid.,* p. 33.
[40]*Ibid.,* p. 267.
[41]*Ibid.,* p. 34.

of habit as embodied in the workings of imagination, for the dramatic nature of the world is reflected and recorded by the dramatic movement of habit.

Dewey cites the following line from Keats with obvious enthusiasm: "The simple imaginative mind may have its rewards in the repetitions of its own silent workings coming continually on the Spirit with a fine suddenness."[42] Although he does not make it explicit at this point, it is apparent that Dewey believes the structures of imagination—habits—to be indeed "silent" in their workings. As he says: "The more suavely efficient a habit the more unconsciously it operates."[43] Thus, although the drama of habit may be played out on the level of conscious, thematic experience, its sources are what Dewey variously refers to as unconscious or subconscious. Habits are, for Dewey, always silent and always present. They are, as Merleau-Ponty says, "anonymous."

---

[42]*Ibid.,* p. 33.
[43]*Human Nature,* p. 178.

Chapter II

HAVING AN EXPERIENCE

Merleau-Ponty is of course in essential agreement with Husserl in holding that object (noema) and intentional act (noesis) are strictly correlative. Both philosophers share a common understanding in their belief that

> consciousness is not first something in itself and then enters also into relationship to something else. The relationship to the other enters into the very essence of the conscious act. Thus, it follows that consciousness is codetermined by the term to which it is related.[1]

Merleau-Ponty, however, does not agree with Husserl's emphasis on intentionality's conscious, cognitive aspects. For this reason, Merleau-Ponty makes it clear in the Preface to the *Phenomenology of Perception* that his major concern is with what Husserl called operative intentionality, "that which produces the natural and antepredicative unity of the world and of our life, being apparent in our desires, our evaluations and in the landscape we see, more clearly than in objective knowledge, and furnishing the text which our knowledge tries to translate into precise language."[2] Clearly, then, Merleau-Ponty does not deny either the existence or importance of conscious, cognitive intentionality. His purpose is to show that man is a sense-giving being on a level of experience which precedes, or is prior to, the conscious positing of distinct objects of cognitive awareness.

Merleau-Ponty develops his theory of pre-objective (preceding distinct objects of cognition and consciousness) intentionality primarily through an extended consideration of the sense-giving capacity of the habitual body. Through the habits of the body (and by "body" Merleau-Ponty of course is referring to the body as subject, the single reality of body-mind, the material and the spiritual), an intentional synthesis

---

[1]Kwant, *The Phenomenological Philosophy of Merleau-Ponty*, p. 154.
[2]*Phenomenology*, p. xviii.

25

takes place which is "anonymous"; organic habits provide the dialectic of body and world with horizons or contexts of acquired, funded, meanings. Such meanings are not, however, the result of conscious, cognitive intentions, because these intentions themselves depend upon the pre-objective meanings of habit for their own sense. All acts—perceptual, cognitive, motor—take "advantage of work already done, of a general synthesis constituted once and for all, and this is what I mean when I say that I perceive with my body or my senses, since my body and my sense are precisely that familiarity with the world born of habit, that implicit or sedimentary body of knowledge."[3] Habits are anonymous because they are pre-objective phenomena. For both Dewey and Merleau-Ponty, habits are the structures of the organism's "silent workings." Hence, the notion of habit offers a "middle term between presence and absence."[4] Habits are absent in the sense that their functioning is silent, impersonal; they provide a pre-objective context of meanings which are taken for granted by the subject, but which nevertheless may become the object of explicit conscious concern if their functioning becomes greatly problematical. It is in this sense that habits are always implicitly present in human experience and potentially present as an explicit text of conscious cognition.

Habits are, for Merleau-Ponty, the ground of the "intentional threads" which establish the pact between body and world. On the pre-objective level of experience, that of operative intentionality, habits *are* the "intentional threads" which relate body and world in one system or structure. Habits constitute what Merleau-Ponty calls the "intentional arc." He writes:

> The life of consciousness—cognitive life, the life of desire or perceptual life—is subtended by an "intentional arc" which projects round about us our past, our future, our human setting, our physical, ideological and moral situation, or rather which results in our being situated in all these respects. It is this intentional arc which brings about the unity of the senses, of intelligence, of sensibility and motility. And it is this which "goes limp" in illness."[5]

---

[3]*Ibid.*, p. 238.
[4]*Ibid.*, p. 80.
[5]*Ibid.*, p. 136.

If the intentional arc "goes limp" in illness, this means that the integration or interpenetration of habits has been destroyed. Then one of two possibilities might occur. It may happen that no habit or configuration of habits is sufficiently strong to maintain some tension between self and world, in which case vitally having and being in situations is made almost impossible. The other possibility is that one habit may become dominant and thus prevent having and being in substantially different situations, in a qualitative sense. The habits of the human body "weave round it a human environment,"[6] and when these habits lose at least a minimal level of integration, the self loses the capacity of carrying on the interaction or dialectic of self and world in a manner which contributes to the growth and expansion of present habits. When the tension of the intentional arc is disrupted, the body's manner of being in situations is transformed, and sometimes any manner of being is rendered impossible.

If the experience of illness involves a loss of integration of organic habits and a resulting loss of integration with the environment, then aesthetic experience is an intensification of the integration of habits and also an intensification of the organism's integration with the environment. Through the experience of works of art

> there are released old, deep-seated habits or engrained organic "memories"; yet these old habits are deployed in new ways, ways in which they are adapted to a more completely integrated world so that they themselves achieve a new integration. Hence the liberating, expansive power of art.[7]

In "Having an Experience," Dewey argues that it is not only in the face of works of art that the integration of habits and integration of self and world take place. Any experience which is "*an* experience" involves the same sort of habit and self-world integration. When a person has *an* experience, one marked by wholeness, completeness, and unity, habits operate in such a manner that the experience is "integrated within and demarcated in the general stream of experience from other experiences."[8] Starting with "conditions of resistance and conflict," the

---

[6]*Ibid.*, p. 327.
[7]John Dewey, "Affective Thought," *Philosophy and Civilization* (New York: Minton, Balch and Company, 1931), p. 121.
[8]Dewey, *Art as Experience,* p. 35.

experience moves from its inception toward its close or consummation. This "forming" of *an* experience as it moves from inception to close is the forming of a new integration or configuration of organic habits. The experience is *an* experience, an integrated, unified whole, because in interaction with the world, the habits constituting the self are formed into a new whole or configuration.

Habits in interaction with the environment qualify the forming experience or situation with what Dewey calls a "pervasive quality." This pervasive quality constitutes the unity or integrity of the situation as experienced by the organism. Dewey is quite emphatic that "this unity is neither emotional, practical, or intellectual, for these terms name distinctions that reflection can make within it."[9] Dewey is claiming here that the pervasive quality of a situation is not the result of emotional, practical, or intellectual habits, taken singly or additively, As he says: "The experience was not a sum of these different characters; they were lost in it as distinctive traits."[10] The pervasive quality which characterizes an experience which has been had is the result of the integration or interpenetration of habits into a total configuration. The pervasive quality is a correlate of the pervasive influence of each habit upon every other habit.

Although the pervasive quality of a situation is not the result of emotional habits taken in isolation from other habits, pervasive quality is, according to Dewey, emotional. He writes:

> Emotion is the moving and cementing force. It selects what is congruous and dyes what is selected with its color, thereby giving qualitative unity to materials externally disparate and dissimilar. It thus provides unity in and through the varied parts of an experience. When the unity is of the sort already described, the experience has esthetic character even though it is not, dominantly, an esthetic experience.[11]

At first glance, it seems as if Dewey has involved himself in a contradiction. He first says that the quality which pervades and unifies an experience is "neither emotional, practical, nor intellectual." He later says that this unifying and pervasive quality is emotional in nature.

---

[9]*Ibid.*, p. 37.
[10]*Ibid.*
[11]*Ibid.*, p. 42.

Dewey here is not contradicting himself, but instead is attempting to establish the pre-objective nature of pervasive quality. Habits are pre-objective phenomena, and qualities also are not experienced as the objects of a knowing consciousness. As Bernstein says:

> Qualities are not directly known, but they are directly experienced, felt, or had. The importance of this distinction between *knowing* and *having* cannot be underestimated, for Dewey . . . has emphasized that we encounter or experience the world in ways that are not primarily cognitive.[12]

The pervasive quality of a situation, a quality which reflects the integrated or (in exceptional cases) unintegrated functioning of emotional, practical, and intellectual habits, is not experienced as an object of cognitive awareness. It is "had" or "felt" by the organism; it is, according to Merleau-Ponty, "lived" rather than known.

Bernstein certainly does not overstate his point when he says that Dewey's theory of quality is "one of the most original and basic features of Dewey's philosophy."[13] Qualitative immediacy forms the basis for understanding not only Dewey's distinction between knowing and having, but also his contextualism, his anti-dualism, his theory of inquiry, and his ethics. Peculiarly, however, Bernstein fails to show that the qualitative is ultimately a function of the habitual. Although this failure is a common characteristic of much writing on Dewey,[14] it is not any less unfortunate since it contributes to the general neglect of the role of habit in Dewey's philosophy. Although it was clear to Dewey, it is not equally clear to his interpreters and critics that if qualities are immediately felt, had, or experienced, they must be the result of a process which is itself not an instance of conscious knowing or thinking. Although Bernstein is correct in saying that "qualities as experienced belong to a situation or context,"[15] he fails to take account of the fact that the situation itself is a product of the interaction of pre-objective

---

[12]*John Dewey* (New York: Washington Square Press, Inc., 1966), p. 93.

[13]Richard J. Bernstein (ed.), *John Dewey on Experience, Nature, and Freedom* (New York: Liberal Arts Press, 1960), p. 176.

[14]For evidence of this, see George R. Geiger, *John Dewey in Perspective: A Reassessment* (New York: McGraw-Hill Book Company, 1958), p. 29. See also S. Morris Eames, "Primary Experience in the Philosophy of John Dewey," *The Monist*, XLVIII (July, 1964).

[15]*John Dewey*, p. 94.

habit and environment. In the same sense that a habit may be both present and absent, a situation is "taken for granted, 'understood,' or implicit in all propositional symbolization."[16] Without habits which provide taken for granted meanings, there would be no self to be in a situation. Without an habitual self, there can be no experienced situations.

It might be argued that although habits are necessary for the possibility of being in a situation, it is still not clear that Dewey was claiming that qualities are a function of habit, even if qualities are always qualities of situations. That Dewey is claiming precisely this point is clear from the example he gives of someone who, walking on the shore of England, sees a promontory and remarks how much it is like one in Wales. Dewey rejects Bradley's explanation that by contiguity, the form of the promontory now seen is taken to be identical to the form of the absent promontory, with the result that the presently seen promontory "suggests" the absent promontory. Dewey rejects this explanation because "identity of pattern, arrangement of form is something that can be apprehended only *after* the other promontory has been suggested, by comparison of the two objects."[17] Dewey puts the matter even more tersely, saying, " 'identity' seems to be the result rather than the antecedent of the association."[18] How, then, are these similar or identical forms associated? Dewey's answer is that "the only way that form or pattern can operate as an immediate link is by the mode of a directly experienced *quality,* something present and prior to and independent of all reflective analysis, something of the same nature which controls artistic construction." This quality is immediately felt and then "made explicit or a term of thought in the idea of another promontory."[19]

What Bernstein and others tend to neglect in their discussions of the qualitative, is that the pervasive quality of a situation is the result of a process of qualification. Association can be intelligently explained only when the self is recognized as a sense-giving being prior to the positing of distinct objects of reflective consciousness. The basis of such pre-objective sense-giving, and thus the basis of association and quality, is habit. Dewey says: "That by which association is effected, by which

16John Dewey, "Qualitative Thought," in Bernstein (ed.), *John Dewey on Experience, Nature, and Freedom,* p. 181.
17*Ibid.,* p. 195.
18*Ibid.,* p. 194.
19*Ibid.,* p. 195.

suggestion and evocation of a distinct object of thought is brought about, is some acquired modification of the organism, usually designated habit."[20] Although Randall too, tends to neglect the role of habit in Dewey's theory of quality, he shows with great skill that "qualities are the outcome of a process of qualification,"[21] wherein the powers contained in the "funded past experience" of the organism cooperate with (in Dewey's terms, interact with) the powers of things seen, heard, touched, and so on. The result is a uniquely, pervasively qualified situation. Thus, Randall makes explicit what is implicit in Dewey: pervasive quality is an outcome of the active participation of both organism and environment in the creation or constitution of a situation. What Randall fails to indicate is that for Dewey, the organism's manner of "cooperating" in the establishment of a pervasive quality is based upon his past experiences as embodied in organic habits.

Dewey is saying, then, that the constitution of the whole precedes association, and this constitution is the work of pre-reflective, pre-conscious habit. Merleau-Ponty, of course, argues exactly the same point. He says: "There are not arbitrary data which set about combining into a thing because *de facto* proximities or likenesses cause them to associate; it is, on the contrary, because we perceive a grouping as a thing that the analytical attitude can then discern likenesses or proximities."[22] Merleau-Ponty does not wish to, in Dewey's words, "offer the problem as a solution," and therefore, he criticizes Wertheimer's laws of contiguity and resemblance "as bringing back the associationist's objective contiguity and resemblance in the rôle of constitutive principles of perception."[23] Contiguity, resemblance, and similarity do not constitute the forms of perception; they do not possess, according to Dewey, "causal efficacy," and to assume that they do is, he says, "to utter meaningless words."

Merleau-Ponty offers an illustration which clarifies his and Dewey's arguments rather well. Walking along the shore towards a ship which has run aground, there will be a moment when the funnel or masts, which have been merged into the forest surrounding the sand dune, will,

---

[20]*Ibid.,* p. 192.
[21]John Herman Randall, Jr., *Nature and Historical Experience: Essays in Naturalism and in The Theory of History* (New York: Columbia University Press, 1958), p. 283.
[22]*Phenomenology,* p. 16.
[23]*Ibid.*

according to Merleau-Ponty, "suddenly become part of the ship, and indissolubly fused with it." Merleau-Ponty says that my recognition of the funnel or masts as being the upper part of a ship is not the result of some combination or association of perceived resemblances or proximities. The form of the upper part of a ship is imminent in the perception of the funnel or masts which sees them as embedded in the forest. This form is, however, imminent only as a "tension" or "vague expectation." Merleau-Ponty writes:

> The unity of the object is based on the foreshadowing of an imminent order which is about to spring upon us a reply to questions merely latent in the landscape. It solves a problem set only in the form of a vague feeling of uneasiness, it organizes elements which up to that moment did not belong to the same universe and which, for that reason, as Kant said with profound insight, could not be associated.[24]

It seems clear that Merleau-Ponty is describing the functioning of habits. As I approach the ship, my habits solicit[25] a response from the perceived scene, and I perceive the funnel or masts as part of the forest. However, the forms of the funnel or masts themselves solicit a response from my habitual meanings, and the result is a "vague feeling of uneasiness" as my habits attempt, quite pre-reflectively and pre-consciously, to make explicit what is initially only an "imminent order." Through one's habits, indeterminate phenomena are transformed into determinate objects; the unity of the object is achieved by one's pre-objective sense-giving power, a power derived from habit.

Although it is commonly recognized that Dewey's theory of quality is fundamental to his entire philosophical effort, it is not commonly recognized that the importance of quality is a derived importance. Pervasive quality is the result or outcome of qualification; a situation is pervasively qualified because the past experiences of the organism, embodied in its habits, interact with present conditions. The result is a situation possessing a pervasive quality which is immediately and pre-reflectively, pre-consciously "had" or "felt" by the organism. Through

---

[24]*Ibid.*, p. 17.

[25]It should be noted that the verb solicit is derived from the Latin *sollicitus,* a combination of *sollus,* meaning whole, and *citus,* pp. of *ciere,* meaning to set in motion. Through the functioning of habits, wholes (experiencing-experienced, noesis-noema) are set in motion.

habits the funded meanings of past experiences are retained for use in present experiences. Thus, habit and quality are responsible for more than simply the association of a promontory in England with one in Wales; they are responsible for the recognition of any promontory *as* a promontory. "By some physiological process, not exactly understood at present but to which the name 'habit' is given, the net outcome of prior experiences gives a dominant quality, designated 'promontory,' to a perceived existence."[26] For an organism possessed of certain habits, the perception of a promontory does not require reflective or even conscious deliberation; the acquired meanings of the past are immediately present in one's habits, and thus the perception of the promontory occurs on a pre-objective level of experience. As Merleau-Ponty says: "The *de facto* past is not imported into present perception by a mechanism of association, but arrayed in present consciousness itself."[27]

Dewey and Merleau-Ponty are both attempting to establish what Langan calls "a new notion of synthesis,"[28] whereby the synthesizing act (experiencing) and the synthesized (experienced) express man's pre-reflective, pre-conscious sense-giving existence. As early as 1906, Dewey recognized that there was an "existential mode of organization" which "is not the work of reason or thought, unless 'reason' be stretched beyond all identification."[29] Dewey is here implying what Merleau-Ponty makes explicit: memory cannot be counted on to explain how the past is present because, like the attempt to explain association on the basis of similarity, appeals to memory "offer the problem as a solution." Merleau-Ponty says:

Before any contribution by memory, what is seen must at the present moment so organize itself as to present a picture to me in which I can recognize my former experiences. Thus the appeal to memory presupposes what it is supposed to explain: the patterning of data, the imposition of meaning on a chaos of sense-data.[30]

[26]Dewey, "Qualitative Thought," p. 197.
[27]*Phenomenology,* p. 19.
[28]Thomas Langan, *Merleau-Ponty's Critique of Reason* (New Haven, Conn.: Yale University Press, 1966), pp. 12-16.
[29]"Experience and Objective Idealism," *The Influence of Darwin on Philosophy* (Bloomington: Indiana University Press, 1910), p. 208. (Hereafter referred to as "Objective Idealism.")
[30]*Phenomenology,* p. 19.

Merleau-Ponty is saying that before a present experience can recall a past experience, it must possess sufficient form, organization, and meaning in order to recall one memory rather than another. What is the basis of such organization? Dewey is clear and emphatic in his response to this question. He affirms that "*as organizations,* as established, effectively controlling arrangements of objects in experience, their mark is that they are not thoughts, but habits, customs of action."[31]

Although Dewey at this point is not concerned to elaborate upon their logical relationship to each other, it is apparent that he is offering a dramatic theory of emotion and quality to complement his dramatic theory of habit. He says: "All emotions are qualifications of a drama and they change as the drama develops."[32] Dewey is referring here to the drama inherent in a situation or "complex experience" where habits form the pre-objective horizon or field of meanings which serves as the context for the thematic text of focal consciousness. In the same way that any particular moment of a drama derives its meaning from its relationship to the total context of the action, so also does an experience depend upon a context of implicit habitual meanings for its sense and order. With respect to emotion, Dewey is not merely claiming that the sense of an emotion is dependent upon some context. He is asserting that the emotion cannot be divorced from its context because it is an outcome or result of that situational context. To illustrate his point, Dewey uses the example of two people who are said to "fall in love at first sight." The drama of such a situation is undeniable; the quickening of one's senses, the delicate and exquisite tension, the promise of fulfillment, all these qualities and more combine to make the situation dramatic. Yet, Dewey wishes to insist that what the lovers "fall into is not a thing of that instant." Their first sight of each other is a union of two histories, histories which are embodied in their respective habitual bodies. The emotion they experience is not "a sort of entity that enters full-made upon the scene, an entity that may last a long time or a short time, but whose duration, whose growth and career, is irrelevant to its nature."[33] No drama is without a career, and neither is any emotion without a history; through our habits we live our past, and through our habits we transcend the past.

---

[31]"Objective Idealism," pp. 209-10.
[32]*Art as Experience,* p. 41.
[33]*Ibid.*

In claiming that "emotions are qualifications of a drama," Dewey was in effect challenging the atomism of traditional empiricism or any other theory which fails to respect the operative intentionality which is at the heart of the pact between self and world. Emotions are a particular reflection of the irreducible implication of self and world. Dewey draws two conclusions from this way of viewing emotion. Because emotions are not elemental but dramatic in nature, Dewey says that "experience is emotional but there are no separate things called emotion in it."[34] Secondly, "emotions are attached to events and objects in their movement."[35] Dewey is making quite clear the intentional nature of emotion. He agrees that emotions belong to a self, but it must be remembered that habits constitute the self, and for this reason emotions participate in the intentional structure of experience. The jump accompanying the occurrence of a sudden noise is not, according to Dewey, an emotional state. It is merely an automatic reflex. In order for fright or shame to become emotional

> they must become part of an inclusive and enduring situation that involves concern for objects and their issues. The jump of fright becomes emotional fear when there is found or thought to exist a threatening object that must be dealt with or escaped from.[36]

Dewey is arguing here that in order for the organism to experience the emotion of fear, the organism must first be implicated in a fearful situation where its habits and the environment interact in such a manner that the situation is pervasively qualified by the emotion of fear. The startled jump at the sound of the noise is not fear because there is no tension or distance between the experiencing and the experienced. In short, there is no drama.

To illustrate what he means by a truly dramatic situation, Dewey uses the example of the relationship between an applicant for a position and an interviewer. On the one hand, the interview may proceed quite mechanically with the interviewer asking set questions and the applicant answering them. Dewey says that such an interview resembles "an exercise in bookkeeping." However, this need not be the case; it

[34]*Ibid.*, p. 42.
[35]*Ibid.*
[36]*Ibid.*

is possible that "an interplay may take place in which a new e
ence develops."[37] How is such an experience best described?
says that neither ledger-entries or a treatise on economics or soc
can adequately deal with the unity of such an experience. It is
again in drama or fiction that Dewey seeks and finds the means
by a particular situation or experience can best be understood. Th
plicant-interviewer situation is dramatic; it is, Dewey says, "fr
with suspense." The drama of the situation stems from the dra
habit. There is suspense and uncertainty as every word and gest
both persons finds a place in the tensed configuration of the o
habits. Furthermore, every word and gesture is the result of some ha
functioning. Thus, the sharing of meanings between interviewe
applicant establishes them, similar to the savage hunter and his q
as participants in what Dewey calls a "single tension." Their "inter
as Dewey terms it, is dramatic because they are both vitally impl
in a situation which is an intensification of the normal or ordinary
tioning of their habits. Hence, in reaching a consummation "throu
connected series of varied incidents," the situation is both drama
and aesthetically qualified.

In the last section of "Having an Experience," Dewey is con
to emphasize the constitutive nature of perception. Since percep
a function of habit, it is not surprising that Dewey should consi
as an active, creative capacity. Furthermore, perception for Dew
for Merleau-Ponty, is a pre-objective phenomenon. Through ha
particular perception may contain much cognitive reference, bu
perception is not, according to both philosophers, a distinct kno
or intellectual affair. Dewey writes:

> Until the artist is satisfied in perception with what he is do-
> ing, he continues shaping and reshaping. The making comes t
> an end when its result is experienced as good—and that exper
> ence comes not by mere intellectual and outside judgment bu
> in direct perception.[38]

Dewey is saying here, as he has said so often, that the relationship
tween self and world in an aesthetic experience is not an affair

---

[37]*Ibid.*, p. 43.
[38]*Ibid.*, p. 49.

᾽ or knowledge. According to Dewey: "Knowing is a connection
.ngs which depends upon other and more primary connections be-
a self and things."[39] Merleau-Ponty agrees with Dewey, saying:
ective thought itself draws on the non-reflective, and presents it-
; an explicit expression of non-reflective consciousness."[40]
In aesthetic experience, the doing and undergoing which is con-
ve of the situation is not a reflective, consciously deliberate proc-
῀he doing and undergoing of both artist and perceiver offer to
ɔtion an "immediate sense" as to whether the perceived objects
ɑrmoniously related or not. This "sense" or immediate meaning is
ɔle because the "whole being" is implicated in the situation. In
tic experience, "hand and eye . . . are but instruments through
the entire live creature, moved and active throughout, operates."[41]
entire live creature" is present with his "whole being" in percep-
᾽f the aesthetic; all his habits are implicated in the constitution of
sthetic experience. What Dewey wishes to emphasize is that the
of perception which characterizes aesthetic experience is not
ɪ, but rather, felt. It is the result of the integrated functioning of
habits whereby both artist and viewer constitute an experience
is whole or coherent in direct perception, but which develops and
ɔs as it is constituted.
t was clear to Dewey that the habits of the artist must, and do,
a union of doing and undergoing where even the undergoing ex-
ɔs the constitutive nature of habit. In other words, Dewey believed
ɪnost people could see the sense in which artistic production is
῀e active affair, involving both habits of mind and body. Dewey
ɔt so certain, however, that it was equally clear to people that
etic perception or viewing is also a constitutive process, one which
creative as the actual creation of a painting or novel. Dewey is
ɪging the notion that aesthetic experience is best described in terms
sive contemplation where one assumes an "aesthetic attitude" of
᾽ɔ receptivity. Dewey wishes to insist, on the contrary, that "re-
ɪty is not passivity. It, too, is a process consisting of a series of

᷈9"Epistemological Realism: The Alleged Ubiquity of the Knowledge Rela-
᷉ Essays in Experimental Logic (New York: Dover Publications, Inc., 1916),
῀6. (Hereafter referred to as "Epistemological Realism.")
40Phenomenology, p. 289.
41Dewey, Art as Experience, p. 50.

responsive acts that accumulate toward objective fulfillment."[42] Dewey
is making the same point as Merleau-Ponty, who says: "My eye fo
me is a certain power of making contact with things, and not a scree
on which they are projected."[43] When perception in general fails t
realize its constitutive power and instead functions as a screen, Dewey
says that there is not perception, but instead mere recognition. He
writes:

> Recognition is perception arrested before it has a chance to
> develop freely. In recognition, there is a beginning of an act
> of perception. But this beginning is not allowed to serve the
> development of a full perception of the thing recognized. It
> is arrested at the point where it will serve some *other* purpose,
> as we recognize a man on the street in order to greet or avoid
> him, not so as to see him for the sake of seeing what is there.[44]

In recognition, there is no tension between the constituting and the
constituted; there is reliance upon a stereotype or scheme which is ap
plied like a stencil to the present experience.

Dewey appears to be saying that when a habit serves merely as
the basis for "bare identification," then we have an example of hab
as it is customarily conceived, i.e., as a rut, groove, or mechanic
routine. Such a conception is, of course, the opposite of how Dewe
thought of habit. Nevertheless, he was the first to admit that hab
can become mere ruts or grooves when there is a lack of interpenetr
tion of cognitive, perceptual, motor, and all of one's other habi
Without such interpenetration, there cannot be "an act of reconstruct
doing" whereby recognition develops into perception. Such percepti
"involves the cooperation of motor elements even though they rem
implicit and do not become overt, as well as cooperation of all fun
ideas that may serve to complete the new picture that is forming
Whether one's habits are typically poorly integrated, or whether o
particular occasion one does not allow the opportunity for them
achieve an integrated functioning, the result is still the same; lack
any sort of tension among themselves, habits fail to establish suffic

---

[42]*Ibid.*, p. 52.
[43]*Phenomenology*, pp. 278-79.
[44]Dewey, *Art as Experience*, p. 52.
[45]*Ibid.*, p. 53.

resistance or tension between constituting and the constituted, with the result that the new is assimilated to the old.

Dewey is a pains to emphasize the necessity of a "continuous interaction" between the "total organism" and perceived objects, if there is to be aesthetic experience. He writes:

> Perception is an act of the going-out of energy in order to receive, not a withholding of energy. To steep ourselves in a subject-matter we have first to plunge into it. When we are only passive to a scene, it overwhelms us and, for lack of answering activity, we do not perceive that which bears us down. We must summon energy and pitch it at a responsive key in order to *take* in.[46]

It is difficult to imagine a more precise statement of the phenomenological notion of intentionality. Dewey combines both operative, pre-objective intentionality, and conscious intentionality in this description of perception. Through the functioning of pre-reflective, pre-conscious habits, one is capable of being in and having a perceptual situation wherein a scene solicits a certain range of response from our habits, and our habits in turn "answer" the solicitation of the scene with a solicitation of their own. According to Calvin O. Schrag:

> Experience in its dynamic unfolding shows itself as an organic complex of vectors which bind together its world-manifesting constituents. The constituents of world experience (experiencer-experiencing-figure-with-background) achieve their connections and conjunctions in a vectorial flow which binds the constituents together into meaningful wholes.[47]

One of the profound advantages of Dewey's notion of habit is that it offers a means of understanding the phenomenological notion of intentionality without resorting to the use of such highly metaphorical concepts as "vectors." The pact, interaction, or dialectic of self and world is bound together by habits; they are the vectors which function as the "meaning-bearing connectives" which establish the reciprocal implication of self and world in all situations.

When Dewey's notion of habit and interaction are understood from the phenomenological standpoint of pre-reflective intentionality,

---

[46]*Ibid.*
[47]*Experience and Being,* p. 83.

it is perfectly clear what Dewey means by his statement that "to perceive, a beholder must *create* his own experience.[48] To perceive, not merely recognize, a work of art, the total organism must constitute the constituted object. If the total organism is not implicated in the constitution of the object, then there will be insufficient resistance or tension between the constituting and the constituted, with the result that there will be no "gathering together of details and particulars physically scattered into an experienced whole."[49] Unless the total configuration of the beholder's habits provides sufficient resistance to the perceived object, it will be assimilated by an isolated habit, thus eliminating the possibility of an "integrated complete experience." The integration of self and world implicit in aesthetic experience is clearly dependent upon the integration of the habitual body. And as Dewey next shows, the habitual body has as its most valuable characteristic, the power of expression.

---

[48] *Art as Experience*, p. 54.
[49] *Ibid.*

CHAPTER III

EXPRESSIVE ACTS AND OBJECTS

Bernstein has remarked that "Having an Experience" "recasts Dewey's entire philosophy of experience."[1] Such an assertion is undeniable, yet it would be mistaken to overemphasize the significance of that chapter as it functions in *Art as Experience,* as well as to exaggerate its place in Dewey's philosophy of experience. If "Having an Experience" is as profound as Bernstein seems to think it is, its profundity is derivative or at least dependent upon a crucial assumption. This assumption is that habits are expressive: having an experience is a demonstration or display of the expressive nature of habits. To understand in what sense Dewey conceived of habit as being expressive, it is necessary to briefly consider Merleau-Ponty's notion of the body as expression.

For Merleau-Ponty, the act of expression—whether perceptual, linguistic, or motor—is the structuring of a field of meanings. He says:

> Every perception, every action which presupposes it, in short every use of the human body, is already a *primordial expression*—not that derivative work which substitutes for the thing expressed a group of signs given as from elsewhere with their meanings and the directions for their use, but the first operation which initially constitutes the signs as signs; i.e., makes the thing expressed inhabit them by the sole means of the eloquence of their arrangement and their configuration; implants a meaning into what before had none; and which, therefore, far from being exhausted in the moment it takes place, inaugurates an order, and founds an institution or tradition. . . .[2]

---

[1]*John Dewey on Experience, Nature, and Freedom,* p. 150.
[2]Merleau-Ponty, quoted by Eugene F. Kaelin, *An Existentialist Aesthetic: The Theories of Sartre and Merleau-Ponty* (Madison: University of Wisconsin Press, 1966), p. 276.

Every act of expression is a "first operation" whereby the sedimented past of the organism, as embodied in its habits, is taken up by the present situation and accordingly restructured. Langan says that "every new configuration is but a rearrangement of a field structured in the configurations of the past, hence the unexpected coming-to-the-fore of points left on the horizons by previous ones, hence the endless possibility of new configurations taking off from the last one, permitting further discovery of other points latent in the original field but left on the horizons by previous configurations."[3] An act of expression is a fixing or crystallization of habitual meanings. It is a fusion of past and present.

Considered from the perspective of Merleau-Ponty, the act of expression is the realization or actualization of acquired meanings which exist as the horizon or context of explicit acts of reflective consciousness. The human body is expressive in many ways because its sense-giving capacities are not restricted to any one modality of experience; meanings have been sedimented in the form of perceptual habits, motor habits, linguistic habits, and all of the other habits of the organism. Not only is the body-mind capable of a wide range of expressive possibilities, but indeed any particular expressive act (perceptual, motor, linguistic, and so on) incorporates into itself at least some of the meanings which exist as the anonymous and generalized habits of the human body. Expressive acts, whether aesthetic or nonaesthetic, are creative in the fundamental sense that habits themselves are creative, sense-constituting phenomena. An expressive act structures the field of habitual meanings; through expression, meanings undergo constant reorganization as new configurations or structures of habits replace older ones. It is because of the expressive capacities of the body-mind, capacities founded upon the functioning of habits, that the human being is capable of expansion and refinement of present meanings.

When viewed phenomenologically, Dewey's theory of expression can be properly understood and appreciated. Not surprisingly, he begins his discussion of expression by noting that an "impulsion" is a movement of the "whole organism." He is almost repetitious in his insistence that an impulsion is a function of the "organism in its entirety," of the "whole self," of the "organism as a whole."[4] Clearly, Dewey

---

[3]*Merleau-Ponty's Critique of Reason,* p. 84.
[4]*Art as Experience,* p. 58.

wishes to emphasize that the act of expression depends upon the entire field of habitual meanings for its sense and direction. An impulsion meets resistance from the environment; the resulting tension is alleviated through a "transformation of energy into thoughtful action, through assimilation of meanings from the background of past experiences." The action is expressive because the union or fusion of past and present is not a mechanical addition of different qualities, but instead is a dramatic appearance of a new order. Dewey says that "the junction of the new and old is not a mere composition of forces, but is a re-creation in which the old, the 'stored,' material is literally revived, given new life and soul through having to meet a new situation."[5]

This action of the past on the present and the action of present on the past is, according to Dewey, "all the elements needed to define expression."[6] The central role of habit in this process is unmistakable since it is through the functioning of habit that the past is present; also, it is because one's history is embodied in habits that the personal past is to some extent accessible to present influence and direction. In the act of expression, the elements which come from prior experience "proceed from the subconscious, not cold or in shapes that are identified with particulars of the past, not in chunks and lumps, but fused in the fire of internal commotion."[7] Dewey is saying here that the field of habitual meanings, when described during the moments of impulsion and inspiration, evidences a high degree of fusion (interpenetration of habits) and tension. The impulsion is, so to speak, the initial electrical charge which shocks the entire field of habitual meanings. A painter sees a certain scene. An impulsion follows whereby his field of habitual meanings becomes charged with energy. This charge is the initial, dramatic structuring of the field of habitual meanings. This impulsion, this incipient ordering of pre-objective meaning, is inspiration.

Dewey was very firm, however, in holding that inspiration is not something which is complete in itself and which the act of expression mechanically realizes. He says:

> Inspiration . . . is initial. In itself, at the outset, it is still inchoate. Inflamed inner material must find objective fuel upon

---

[5]*Ibid.*, p. 60.
[6]*Ibid.*, p. 61.
[7]*Ibid.*, p. 65.

which to feed. Through the interaction of the fuel with material already afire the refined and formed product comes into existence. The act of expression is not something which supervenes upon an inspiration already complete. It is the carrying forward to completion of an inspiration by means of the objective material of perception and imagery.[8]

In insisting upon the need for continued interaction of self and environment, Dewey is once again affirming the intentional nature of habit, this time by developing the intentional nature of expression. According to Dewey: "Habits are ways of using and incorporating the environment in which the latter has its say as surely as the former."[9] Through acts of expression, founded upon pre-objective, sense-giving habit, an art object is constituted as the result of the reciprocal implication of artist and environment in a developing situation or experience. Because inspiration is merely the initial stage in the development of a complete aesthetic experience, continued expressive acts are required in order to bring the experience to an organized, ordered completion. Through these expressive acts, both the objective physical material and the field of habitual meanings are ordered and formed. Habit and object motivate each other; when both achieve their most complete organization, the experience itself is aesthetically complete.

In view of Dewey's respect for the life of the savage, it is not at all surprising that he should turn to him for further illustration of the basic intentionality of expressive acts. Dewey remarks that

the war dance and the harvest dance of the savage do not issue from within except there be an impending hostile raid or crops that are to be gathered. To generate the indispensable excitement there must be something at stake, something momentous and uncertain—like the outcome of a battle or the prospects of a harvest.[10]

Turmoil and emotion mark the place where impulsion and environment meet. This emotion is an expression of "something momentous and uncertain"; it is basically dramatic. This means that the dramatic nature of the emotion is continuous with the dramatic situation where-

---

[8]*Ibid.*, p. 66.
[9]*Human Nature*, p. 15.
[10]*Art as Experience*, p. 66.

in self and world are constitutive of each other. It must always be remembered that "an emotion is *to* or *from* or *about* something objective, whether in fact or in idea."[11] Dewey is not implying that emotions are, in some sense, objective. He is merely saying that the experienced emotion has an intentional object "whether in fact or in idea," i.e., a certain emotion may have as its intentional object a horse or an idea of a horse. Just as habits are always implicated in, because constitutive of and constituted by, situations, so also is an emotion "implicated in a situation, the issue of which is in suspense and in which the self that is moved in the emotion is vitally concerned."[12] Both habit and emotion are dramatic and intentional; both constitute, and are constituted by, situations.

What Dewey has been attempting to do up to this point is to clarify the concept of emotion in order to better understand its role in expressive acts. He quickly dismisses the notion that it is emotion which is expressed in expressive acts. He puts it succinctly, saying that emotion "is selective of material and directive of its order and arrangement. But it is not *what* is expressed."[13]

When it is understood that "emotion is a perturbation from clash or failure of habit,"[14] then it becomes clearer how emotion functions in expressive acts. When there is an act of expression, habits are in the process of forming and reforming various configurations; in the process, they clash and fail as they respond to, and form, the intentional object. This clash and failure of habit is experienced by the organism as emotion. Since emotion is a function of pre-objective habits, its selective and ordering characteristics possess a facility which is not matched by deliberate, reflective awareness. "An emotion is," Dewey says, "more effective than any deliberate challenging sentinel could be."[15] Once the relationship between habit and emotion is properly understood, it is evident that when Dewey speaks of a failure of emotion in a work of art, he is indicating that the expressive acts of the artist failed to effect an integration of his habits, and hence failed to achieve an integration of the materials.

---

[11]*Ibid.*, p. 67.
[12]*Ibid.*
[13]*Ibid.*, p. 69.
[14]Dewey, *Human Nature*, p. 76.
[15]*Art as Experience*, p. 67.

Having dealt with the place of emotion in expression, Dewey next turns his attention to the relationship between spontaneity and expression. The major point which he is trying to make is that the "most spontaneous outbursts, if expressive, are not overflows of momentary internal pressures."[16] Too often, a spontaneous act is considered to be an event somehow separate from one's past. Frequently, it is said that someone did something "spontaneously," implying that the action is a product of its own existence, i.e., self-contained and unrelated to the history of the subject. To Dewey, such a notion is naive, since the meaning of past experiences are the basis upon which a person spontaneously acts this way rather than another. Spontaneity is not a falsification of the basic temporality of existence. Merleau-Ponty remarks that "the upsurge of a fresh present does not *cause* a heaping up of the past and a tremor of the future; the fresh present is the passage of future to present, and of former present to past, and when time begins to move, it moves throughout its whole length."[17] Dewey's discussion of spontaneity confirms Merleau-Ponty's statement that "since in time being and passing are synonymous, by becoming past, the event does not cease to be."[18]

A spontaneous act, when expressive, is a crystallization of the field of time. The history of a person is embodied in his pre-reflective, preconscious habits. In addition, every habit projects a future, "every habit creates an unconscious expectation."[19] Consequently, every spontaneous expressive action is a dramatization or intensification of the retentive and protentive capacities of habit. Viewed from the standpoint of pre-objective, habitual meaning, the following statement by Dewey takes on an added significance. He says:

> The spontaneous in art is complete absorption in subject matter that is fresh, the freshness of which holds and sustains emotion, Staleness of matter and obtrusion of calculation are the two enemies of spontaneity of expression."[20]

When subject matter is stale, it does not offer sufficient resistance to the habits of the person, and hence no situation is constituted through

---

[16]*Ibid.*, p. 70.
[17]*Phenomenology*, p. 419.
[18]*Ibid.*, p. 420.
[19]Dewey, *Human Nature*, p. 75.
[20]*Art as Experience*, p. 70.

the interaction of habitual body and world. Spontaneous expression is also threatened by calculation, or the deliberate positing of distinct objects of conscious cognition. Spontaneous expression may embody any degree of reflection, and in a certain sense it must, but spontaneous expression as experienced or lived is not a reflective experience.

In his discussion of spontaneity, Dewey, is led to briefly consider unconscious and subconscious experience. At first, it may seem surprising that Dewey should talk about "differring levels of selfhood" and meanings which "sink deep." Dewey had always been very suspicious of the Freudian unconscious, believing that it represented the extent to which functions could be hypostatized and thus lose their functional character. Nevertheless, Dewey never seems to have doubted that there are meanings experienced by the person which are prior to, or precede, conscious formulation. As early as 1916, in his Introduction to *Essays in Experimental Logic,* Dewey indicts the intellectualist for "supposing that no qualities or things at all are present in experience except as objects of some kind of apprehension or awareness." In the same paragraph, Dewey continues his attack upon the intellectualist who "thinks of things as either totally absent from experience or else there as objects of 'consciousness' or knowing."[21] It is quite apparent that even at this point in his development, Dewey recognized the necessity of somehow accounting for the pre-reflective, pre-conscious meanings which seem to play such an extensive role in conscious experience. Dewey developed his explanation in terms of habit, although most commonly he did not designate habit as the structure of pre-objective meanings.

It seemed undeniable to Dewey that "each of us assimilates into himself something of the values and meanings contained in past experiences."[22] This, obviously, is the basis of learning. Yet, not all previously experienced meanings become part of the self. "Some things sink deep, others stay on the surface and are easily displaced." Dewey is saying that not all experienced meanings become habitual. Some "stay on the surface" and others "sink deep." Those meanings which do become pre-objectively habitual support Dewey's claim that

> it is not true that we "forget" or drop into unconsciousness
> only alien and disagreeable things. It is even more true that the

[21]*Essays in Experimental Logic* (New York: Dover Publications, Inc., 1916), p. 3.
[22]*Art as Experience,* p. 71.

things which we have most completely make a part of ourselves, that we have assimilated to compose our personality and
not merely retained as incidents, cease to have a separate,
conscious existence.[23]

It is this stock of taken for granted, pre-objective meanings, meanings
which are not objects of consciousness or knowing, which are the basis
of spontaneous expression.

Dewey is careful to point out, however, that a spontaneous expression is not merely the expression of meanings which have been
retained from previous experiences. Since they are intentional, habits
constitute a situation; an act of expression involves "an intimate union
of the features of present experience with the values that past experience have incorporated in personality."[24] Because my past is generalized
in the form of habits, and because the present circumstance is particular with respect to its characteristics, this "union" or creation of an
experienced situation in an act of spontaneous expression, shows itself to be highly dramatic. The field of habitual meanings, as a "general background or context (*fond*) attaches the particular present configuration of this thing or moment to both the relevant preceding (in
either a spatial or temporal sense) experience and to the relevant experience to come, thereby assuring that it has a sense."[25] "The building up of a truly expressive act"[26] is a dialectic or interaction between
my past as generalized in habits, and the present particular circumstance; it is a dialectic of background and figure. An expressive act is
dramatic because the union or integration of generalized past and particular present is fraught with uncertainty and ambiguity. Langan remarks that "in the kind of tense equilibrium which exists between
figure and background, the alteration of one element, bringing about
as it does a shift in the experience's norm or center, inevitably alters
it sense."[27] Thus, expression is founded upon, and displays, the drama
of habit.

Dewey's statement that "subconscious maturation precedes crea-

---

[23]*Ibid.*
[24]*Ibid.*
[25]Langan, *Merleau-Ponty's Critique of Reason,* p. 34.
[26]Dewey, *Art as Experience,* p. 74.
[27]*Merleau-Ponty's Critique of Reason,* p. 36.

tive production in every line of human endeavor,"[28] is a fair indication of the enormous importance he attributed to pre-objective meaning and experience. In view of the fact that "we perform different acts, each with its own particular result," Dewey is amazed that somehow or other these acts are unified and integrated by the organism. Of course, Dewey had some rather definite ideas as to how acts might be related by the organism. Since acts "all proceed from one living creature they are somehow bound together below the level of intention"[29] (Dewey is not using "intention" in a technical, phenomenological sense). Dewey's use of "somehow" in this sentence is, to some extent, gratuitous, since he was relatively certain that habit was responsible for the unity and integration of the self. No doubt Dewey felt humble in the face of what Merleau-Ponty called "the miracle of related experiences."[30]

When habit is understood and appreciated in all of its complexity, it becomes clearer what the expressions of the artist have in common with those of the scientist. Both forms of expression require "subconscious maturing," wherein the field of habitual meanings, through its dialectic or interaction with intentional objects, is restructured to form new configurations. This maturing is pre-objective; it occurs anonymously and without "deliberate will." Scientists, as well as artists, "press forward toward some end dimly and imprecisely prefigured, groping their way as they are lured on by the identity of an aura in which their observations and reflections swim."[31] In both artist and scientist, the drama of habit results in what Dewey calls "emotionalized thinking"; habits fuse and interpenetrate in such a manner that both persons have "feelings whose substance consists of appreciated meanings or ideas."[32] Hence, the only major difference between artist and scientist is that the intentional objects of their intentional acts typically are different. Nevertheless, both persons rely upon the sense-giving capacity of pre-reflective, pre-conscious habits to provide a general and anonymous horizon or context of taken for granted meanings. Without such an horizon or context, neither artist nor scientist would possess the means whereby he could create any sort of meaning, whether in the form of a novel or an equation.

---

[28]*Art as Experience*, p. 73.
[29]*Ibid.*
[30]*Phenomenology*, p. xx.
[31]Dewey, *Art as Experience*, p. 73.
[32]*Ibid.*

Dewey concludes the chapter on "The Act of Expression" with a reaffirmation that "the building up of a truly expressive act" involves an ordering of objective material as well as an ordering of the "inner" material of images, observations, memories, and emotions. In an act of expression, these orderings are not distinct from each other; each contributes to the progressive realization of the other's completion. As Dewey says, it is "only by progressive organization of 'inner' and 'outer' material in organic connection with each other can anything be produced that is not a learned document or an illustration of something familiar."[33] This basic notion of phenomenological intentionality is at the heart of Dewey's concept of interaction, and thus at the very heart of his entire philosophy. The relationship between expressive act and expressive object is not one of cause and effect. Kwant says:

> The causal interaction can be analyzed in two processes which, strictly speaking, can be understood independently of each other. The concept "causal interaction" is a thought form of certain sciences insofar as they think in an atomistic fashion and want to understand a whole from the standpoint of its elements.[34]

An act of expression is not the sum of two separate processes or two separate systems of causality, since it is an integrated or total process, one which "cannot be dissolved into two independent actions, for the one cause does not merely act on the other but also effects the other's causality which it itself undergoes."[35] Dewey's later use of "transaction" in place of "interaction" is an attempt to once and for all abandon causal thinking, or at least reductive causal thinking, in favor of dialectical thinking whereby the experiencing-experienced, the expressing-expressed, in short, act and object, are mutually constitutive. What Dewey struggled to make clear on so many occasions was that our conscious, reflective dialectic of self and world is founded upon a pre-reflective, pre-conscious dialectic of self and world, one which is derived from habit. Meaning comes into being through the dialectic of self and world, and man is a sense-giving being on the level of pre-objective experience, that of habit.

---

[33]Ibid., p. 75.
[34]The Phenomenological Philosophy of Merleau-Ponty, p. 19.
[35]Ibid.

Dewey begins the chapter on "The Expressive Object" with a reminder that "expression as personal act and as objective result are organically connected with each other."[36] This reminder helps Dewey to place Roger Fry's formalism in perspective. Dewey is in agreement with Fry that a painting is not a representation of "objects as such"; certain lines and colors become "full of meaning" as they are brought into new relationships to each other. Dewey believes that it is because of habit that "lines and color crystallize in this harmony rather than in that." Consequently, the particular way in which line and color are organized is not the result of just the formal properties of the lines and colors:

> It is a function of what is in the actual scene in its interaction with what the beholder brings with him. Some subtle affinity with the current of his own experience as a live creature causes lines and colors to arrange themselves in one pattern and rhythm rather than in another.[37]

The basis of the "affinity" of which Dewey speaks is habit. The potentiality of lines and colors now perceived to be arranged into aesthetically pleasing wholes, depends upon the effectiveness with which the artist's past experiences, embodied in habits, fuse or interpenetrate with present conditions.

This fact that the artist, like any human being, "carries his past in his habitudes and habituations,"[38] is adequate reason for Dewey to reject Fry's contention that the "subject matter" of a work of art is irrelevant to its aesthetic perception. If this were so, "then the meanings of lines and colors would completely replace all meanings that attach to this and any other experience of natural scene."[39] The possibility of this occurring, however, is slight, since one's perception of anything—whether natural scene or abstract painting—is the result of at least a minimal integration of perceptual, motor, and cognitive habits. Consequently, perception involves a range of meanings which far exceeds the "meanings of lines and colors," both in quantity and qualitative richness. Dewey is quite convinced that

[36]*Art as Experience,* p. 82.
[37]*Ibid.,* p. 87.
[38]John Dewey, "Body and Mind," *Philosophy and Civilization* (New York: Minton, Balch and Company, 1931), p. 308.
[39]Dewey, *Art as Experience,* p. 88.

no matter how ardently the artist might desire it, he cannot divest himself in his new perception, of meanings funded from his past intercourse with his surroundings, nor can he free himself from the influence they exert upon the substance and manner of his present seeing. If he could and did, there would be nothing left in the way of an object for him to see.[40]

In his rejection of formalism, Dewey is reasserting the unity, the pre-objective unity, of the human organism. According to Fry, only a portion of one's past is (or should be) present in the object now seen, that portion relevant to the formal properties of lines or colors. Both Dewey and Merleau-Ponty would have considerable difficulty even making sense out of such a claim. Through the functioning of habits, "each present reasserts the presence of the whole past which it supplants, and anticipates that of all that is to come."[41]

Clearly, then, the field of time, as well as the field of habitual meanings, functions as a whole, and therefore the meanings which are operative in a perception are not just, or only, "meanings of lines and colors." The intentional act of the beholder's and artist's perception, itself an expressive act, is a crystallization (in various degrees of intensity) of the entire field of habitual meanings. Without such a minimally integrated intentional act, "there would be nothing left in the way of an object" for artist or beholder to see. To fail to recognize this, as Fry does, is to impoverish the meaning and value of aesthetic experience, as well as to misunderstand the nature of the pre-objective, intentional synthesis which is habit.

Dewey has repeatedly stated that an impulsion must be modified or transformed if it is to gain expressive value. According to him, "there are two modes of collateral and cooperative response" which "explain the expressiveness of the perceived object." The first of these "collateral tendencies" is "the existence of motor dispositions previously formed." It is fairly obvious that "a surgeon, golfer, ball player, as well as a dancer, painter, or violin player has at hand and under command certain motor sets of the body."[42] These "tendencies of action" or habits are "at hand"; indeed, habit is, according to Merleau-Ponty, "knowl-

---

40Ibid., p. 89.
41Merleau-Ponty, *Phenomenology*, p. 420.
42Dewey, *Art as Experience*, p. 97.

edge in the hands."[43] Through the silent functioning of motor habits, "effective lines of motor response" enable the artist to "live" or "have" a situation or experience on a pre-objective level. As Merleau-Ponty says: "When the typist performs the necessary movements on the typewriter, these movements are governed by an intention, but the intention does not posit the keys as objective locations."[44]

Merleau-Ponty uses the example of an organist to show the anonymity and generality of motor habits, to show "how habit has its abode neither in thought nor in the objective body, but in the body as mediator of a world."[45] An experienced organist is capable of playing an organ which he is unfamiliar with, one which has more or fewer stops and manuals than the familiar organ. They even may be differently arranged, but because the organist is possessed of certain habits, he forms a system with the new organ. This capacity is neither the result of new conditioned reflexes, since the organist can achieve a "comprehensive grasp of the instrument" in a relatively short time, nor is it the outcome of an intellectual analysis whereby a plan of the stops, manuals, pedals, and their relationship to each other is committed to "memory." Commenting on the possibility that the organist constructs a plan of the new organ, Merleau-Ponty says:

> During the short rehearsal preceding the concert, he does not act like a person about to draw up a plan. He sits on the seat, works the pedals, pulls out the stops, gets the measure of the instrument with his body, incorporates within himself the relevant directions and dimensions, settles into the organ as one settles into a house.[46]

Thus, through the functioning of the habitual body, the self and the organ come to constitute a situation founded upon pre-reflective, preconscious habits. Habit is both anonymous and general; it provides the horizon or context of taken for granted meanings which thematic acts of cognition and consciousness take up and develop. Habit grounds later, fully developed intellectual acts; in doing so, "habit expresses our

---

[43]*Phenomenology*, p. 144.
[44]*Ibid.*, p. 145.
[45]*Ibid.*
[46]*Ibid.*

power of dilating our being in the world, or changing our existence by appropriating fresh instruments."[47]

The same considerations which apply to the artist with respect to motor habits, also are relevant in connection with the perceiver. Aesthetic perception is, for Dewey, quite dependent upon adequate "motor preparation." To understand and appreciate a perceived object, there must be a "readiness on the part of motor equipment." This "readiness," based upon habit, is why "a surgeon is the one who appreciates the artistry of another surgeon's performance; he follows it sympathetically, though not overtly, in his own body."[48] Because artist and viewer are possessed of an habitual body which is the incarnation of past experiences, present perception is rendered more acute, intense, and meaningful. In view of the importance of the habitual body, it is no exaggeration on Merleau-Ponty's part when he says that "the body is our general medium for having a world."[49]

The second of the two "collateral tendencies" which contributes to the expressiveness of a perceived object, is what Dewey refers to as "funded" meanings from prior experiences. These "funded" meanings, embodied in the organism as habits, "fuse with the qualities directly presented in the work of art."[50] This "fusion" or "blending" of past meanings and present qualities is not a matter of "extraneous suggestions," i.e., certain habitual meanings are not "suggested" by particular and immediate sounds or colors. What Dewey is attempting to do in arguing that past meanings and present qualities form an "internal and intrinsic integration," is to establish the reciprocity of constituting act and constituted object. Habits solicit[51] certain reactions to a perceived object; reciprocally, the perceived object solicits certain responses from the field of habitual meanings. The resulting total solicitation represents a "fusion" or "blending" of the organism's contribution to the interaction and that of the perceived object. This fusion or integration is, according to Dewey, "internal" and "intrinsic." In a highly significant passage in

---

[47]*Ibid.*, p. 143.

[48]Dewey, *Art as Experience*, p. 98.

[49]*Phenomenology*, p. 146.

[50]*Art as Experience*, p. 98. For a typical example of how Dewey's notion of fusion and quality can be reduced to the obvious, see Stephen C. Pepper, "The Concept of Fusion in Dewey's Aesthetic Theory," *The Journal of Aesthetics and Art Criticism*, XII (December, 1953).

[51]See above, page 32, footnote 25.

Essays in Experimental Logic, Dewey explains in what sense perception is an internal and intrinsic relationship between self and object. He says:

> If we take a case of perception, we find upon analysis that, so far as a self or organism is concerned in it at all, the self is, so to say, inside of it rather than outside of it. It would be much more correct to say that a self is contained in a perception than that a perception is presented to a self. That is to say, the organism is involved in the occurrence of the perception in the same sort of way that hydrogen is involved in the happening—producing—of water. We might about as well talk of the production of a specimen of water as a presentation of water to hydrogen as talk in the way we are only too accustomed to talk about perceptions and the organism. When we consider a perception as a case of "apperception," the same thing holds good. Habits enter into the *constitution* of the situation; they are in and of it, not, so far as it is concerned, something outside of it.[52]

Habit and object are not elements or parts which are somehow added to each other thereby forming a whole. They are moments or aspects of a "single tension," one which is formed as an outcome of the dialectic of pre-objective habit and perceived object. Thus, in maintaining that the suggesting and the suggested interpenetrate to form a unity, Dewey was again emphasizing the fundamental intentionality of habit.

In view of the close relationship that has been shown to exist between habit, meaning and expressiveness, it is certainly not surprising that Dewey concludes the chapter of "The Expressive Object" with a brief reiteration of their relationship. He says that "the expressiveness of the object of art is due to the fact that it presents a thorough and complete interpenetration of the materials of undergoing and of action, the latter including a reorganization of matter brought with us from past experience."[53] An object is expressive when it possesses the capacity to solicit a reorganization or reconstruction of my field of habitual meanings. This solicitation is mutual or reciprocal; habit and object contribute to the constitution of a single situation, a "single tension." Likewise, an act is expressive when it involves a crystallization or tensed restructuring of the field of habitual meanings, when these mean-

---

[52]Dewey, "Epistemological Realism," pp. 276-77.
[53]Dewey, *Art as Experience,* p. 103.

ings meet with resistance from some experienced object. Aesthetic experience is an intensification of the intentionality of habit. It is a celebration of meaning, meaning which is constituted out of the centrifugal and centripital capacities of habit. These capacities, opposite yet complementary, are to a large extent the basis of habit's dramatic nature. The tension, suspense, and uncertainty which attend the dialectic of the constituting and the constituted is fundamentally dramatic; as it works toward an integration of the self (conceived of as the general configuration of one's habits) and self and world, tension and ambiguity are never eliminated; instead, they become qualities of new configurations of habits. Thus, expressive acts and objects are an intensification of the drama of habit. When the expressive capacities of habit are thus understood and appreciated, it is seen that there is no exaggeration in Dewey's profound statement that "through habits formed in intercourse with the world, we also inhabit the world."[54]

---

[54]*Ibid.,* p. 104.

CHAPTER IV

FORM AND ORGANIZATION

According to Dewey, when "the self is regarded as something complete and self-contained in isolation, then of course substance and form fall apart."[1] Herein is the heart of the question concerning the primacy of form or content. Self-expression traditionally has been conceived of in one of two ways. Expressive acts have been thought of as some sort of delivering up of complete and determinate products or contents, as matter which merely has to be "ex-pressed" out of the self in order to achieve an independent existence. Acts of expression also have been discussed in terms of the self imposing form on an indifferent matter. Both conceptions are erroneous, and the theories of the relationship between form and content which have been based on them are also mistaken.

Self-expression, whether that of artist or viewer, is a function of the intentionality of the self, when self is taken as the general configuration of one's organic habits during a particular period of time. An act of self-expression is a crystallization, a forming and reforming of the field of habitual meanings in dialectic or interaction with the environment. Neither form or content is primary in any logical sense since content is formed as it comes into being. Hence, there is no deliverance or expulsion of a "ready-made" matter out of the organism and into the world, matter which only incidentally picks up form along the way. Nor is there any imposition of form on some sort of passive, indifferent matter. Matter or content is created or constituted out of the dialectic of intentional act, founded upon habit, and intentional object. Thus, matter is formed as it makes its appearance in the world. Form and content are correlative and contemporaneous; each is a condition of the other's existence.

The correlativity of habit as intentional act and subject matter as intentional object is clearly illustrated in the case of the viewer or per-

---

[1]*Ibid.*, p. 107.

57

ceiver. If the viewer perceives aesthetically, i.e., if his perception is an act of expression and not one of mere recognition, "he will create an experience of which the intrinsic subject matter, the substance, is new."[2] Dewey is saying here that the art object will solicit different responses from different people since the differing habits of people will solicit different responses from the art object. Dewey puts it quite well when he says that

> a new poem is created by every one who reads poetically—not that its *raw* material is original for, after all, we live in the same old world, but that every individual brings with him, when he exercises his individuality, a way of seeing and feeling that in interaction with old material creates something new, something previously not existing in experience.

Every reader brings to a poem his own " 'form,' or manners of response."[3] Dewey certainly is not using "form" in any idealistic sense, but is merely capitalizing on the possible meanings inherent in the phrase "form or manner of response." Each reader forms his response to the poem in a uniquely different manner, based upon the forming and reforming of the field of habitual meanings. The formation of his response is not, however, a case of the imposition of form on the art object. The poem itself makes demands upon the habits of the reader; habits respond to the solicitation of the poem by forming and reforming new configurations at the same time that they are questioning the poem with their own solicitation. There is uncertainty and ambiguity as the habits of the individual and the poem constitute themselves and each other as aspects of a "single tension." Thus, aesthetic experience is fundamentally and inherently dramatic because it is an intensification of the drama, the intentionality, of habit.

Dewey's major concern in "Substance and Form" is to clarify the relationship between sense and meaning, in an effort to show that perceptual experience may embody meanings which are immediately "felt" or "had" by the human organism. Dewey is strongly opposed to that sort of atomism which splits sense qualities and meaning into separate elements which somehow are "associated" by the organism. As he says: "Sense qualities are the carriers of meanings, not as vehicles carry

---

[2]*Ibid.*, p. 108.
[3]*Ibid.*

goods but as a mother carries a baby when the baby is part of her own organism.[4] The relationship between sense and meaning is not external or extraneous; there is no association of them by a " 'synthetic' action of thought." Meaning is immediately present in perception because habits—acquired, funded, or accepted meanings—are constitutive of the perception. Thus it is that any degree of reflection may be embodied in a perception, since the habitual meanings accumulated from past experiences are the means whereby the perceptual situation is constituted. Consequently, to say that habitual meanings are immediately present *in* a perceptual situation is still too external, suggesting as it does, the way in which pencils are in a box. Habitual meanings are constitutive *of* the perceptual situation; in dialectic or interaction with the intentional object, habits form a "single tension." Similarly, an embryonic baby is not merely *in* the mother; it is *of* the mother and, in interaction with her, forms a single system or structure.

Dewey is very emphatic on the point that what is not qualitatively, immediately, and directly experienced, cannot be considered aesthetic experience. "It cannot be asserted too strongly that what is not immediate is not esthetic."[5] The great emphasis which Dewey places on qualitative immediacy is, in effect, a reminder of what he had already made clear in "Qualitative Thought": the qualitative is a function of the habitual. We are capable of directly "feeling" or "sensing" an idea because we possess habits. Before a meaning becomes a thematic idea, it is experienced as a vague, qualitative "feeling"; we have a "sense" of what we wish to say, yet our expression is inadequate to our intention. In this case, the field of habitual meanings—perceptual, motor, linguistic—has not achieved a satisfactory configuration. The sense or direction of the developing meaning is recognizable, but aspects of the field of habitual meanings are still unsettled and hence our verbal utterance does not fully express the total sense which is experienced as an anticipation or expectation.

What Dewey is striving to impress upon the reader is that having a "sense" of something is not limited to just those experiences in which there is development or growth of a vague meaning into an explicit, distinct meaning. Habits provide the horizon or context of pre-

---

[4]*Ibid.*, p. 118.
[5]*Ibid.*, p. 119.

objective meanings which give a distinct idea its immediate "sense" or qualitative "feel." "We cannot grasp," Dewey says, "any idea, any organ of mediation, we cannot possess it in full force, until we have felt and sensed it, as much so as if it were an odor or color."[6] Dewey is attempting to reinforce his position that there is no separation between sense (form) and idea (content). Just as there is no primacy with respect to form or content, similarly there is no primacy in connection with sense and idea. An idea is a meaning transformed by the process of thinking, and "thinking is secreted in the interstices of habits."[7] Perceptions and ideas are both founded on habit, and just as a perception is marked by a distinct qualitative "feel," "different ideas have their different 'feels,' their immediate qualitative aspects."[8] The felt quality of an idea is not merely an incidental characteristic; it is a necessary characteristic, for "whenever an idea loses its immediate felt quality, it ceases to be an idea and becomes, like an algebraic symbol, a mere stimulus to execute an operation without the need of thinking."[9] Thus, meanings are present in an aesthetic experience, but not as "objects of a cognitive regard, themes of an intellectual gesture."[10] Sense and meaning are unified in the pre-objective, non-thematic level of experience upon which habits function.

Dewey saw clearly that this unity of sense and meaning presupposed the unity of the habitual body: "The action of any one sense includes attitudes and dispositions that are due to the whole organism."[11] It must be remembered that Dewey thought of attitudes and dispositions as forms of habit; in discussing their relationship to habit he says, "if we perceive that they denote positive forms of action which are released merely through removal of some counteracting 'inhibitory' tendency, and then become overt, we may employ them instead of the word habit to denote subdued, non-patent forms of the latter."[12] Quite clearly, then, Dewey is saying that habits come to interpenetrate with one another in an intensified manner during aesthetic experience. He writes:

[6]Ibid.
[7]John Dewey, The Public and Its Problems (Chicago: Swallow Press, Inc., 1927), p. 160.
[8]Dewey, Art as Experience, p. 120.
[9]Ibid.
[10]Dewey, "Introduction," Essays in Experimental Logic, p. 4.
[11]Art as Experience, p. 121.
[12]Human Nature, p. 41.

It is not just the visual apparatus but the whole organism that interacts with the environment in all but routine action. The eye, ear, or whatever, is only the channel *through* which the total response takes place. A color as seen is always qualified by implicit reactions of many organs, those of the sympathetic system as well as of touch. It is a funnel for the total energy put forth, not its well-spring. Colors are sumptuous and rich just because a total organic resonance is deeply implicated in them.[13]

The senses of one who perceives aesthetically, like those of the savage, are "sentinels of immediate thought and outposts of action" because the "whole organism," the entire field of habitual meanings, is implicated in the perceptual situation.

Dewey was also aware that the unity of sense and meaning presupposes the continuity of past and present. He writes that the organism

carries past experiences in itself not by conscious memory but by direct charge. This fact accounts for the existence of some degree of expressiveness in the object of every conscious experience.[14]

Every conscious experience involves some solicitation of and by the pre-reflective, pre-conscious field of habitual meanings; for this reason every object of conscious experience possesses some degree of expressiveness. The difference between aesthetic and non-aesthetic experience is that the former involves an intensification of a larger number of habits and their relationship to each other. Dewey remarks that "the scope of a work of art is measured by the number and variety of elements coming from past experiences that are organically absorbed into the perception had here and now."[15] Dewey is not attempting to establish a minimum number of habits which, once activated in a particular experience, entitle it to be designated aesthetic. He is merely reaffirming the fact that habits are organically related to each other; the field of habitual meanings is a Gestalt or configuration where each separate habit affects, however slightly, the entire field, and the total

---

[13]*Art as Experience,* p. 122.
[14]*Ibid.*
[15]*Ibid.,* p. 123.

field affects the quality of each habit. This means that the drama of habit
as exhibited in aesthetic experience is not a function of any one habit,
but instead is a function of the entire tensed field of habits, habits which
have fused or have come to embody each other in response to the
solicitation of the experienced object. Dewey is saying that the more
habits that are vitally involved in the constitution of the aesthetic experience, the greater is its effect upon the self, since habits *are* the
self.

Because of its critical importance, Dewey never tires in reaffirming the unity of the organism. He writes that "when we perceive, by
means of the eyes as causal aids, the liquidity of water, the coldness
of ice, the solidity of rocks, the bareness of trees in winter, it is certain
that other qualities than those of the eye are conspicuous and controlling
in perception."[16] Merleau-Ponty provides substantial support for Dewey's emphasis on the unity of the senses. Merleau-Ponty says:

> The senses intercommunicate by opening on to the structure
> of the thing. One sees the hardness and brittleness of glass, and
> when, with a tinkling sound, it breaks, this sound is conveyed
> by the visible glass. One sees the springiness of steel, the
> ductility of red-hot steel, the hardness of a plane blade, the
> softness of shavings.[17]

Both Dewey and Merleau-Ponty attribute the unity of the senses to
their intentionality, the fact that they open "on to the structure of the
thing." Following a description of W. H. Hudson's "extraordinary sensi-
tiveness to the sensuous surface of the world," Dewey affirms:

> It will be noted that "colors, scents, taste and touch" are not
> isolated. The enjoyment is of the color, feel, and scent of
> *objects*: blades of grass, sky, sunlight and water, birds. The
> sight, smell, touch immediately appealed to are means through
> which the boy's entire being reveled in acute perception of the
> qualities of the world in which he lived—qualities of things
> experienced not of sensation.[18]

Thus, the "thing" or "object" is the intentional correlate of the perceptual act which itself is founded upon the pre-objective intentionality

---

[16]*Ibid.*
[17]*Phenomenology*, p. 229.
[18]*Art as Experience*, p. 125.

of habit. The thing or object solicits a response from the boy's "entire being," i.e., the total field of his habitual meanings. The response may occur through one sense organ, but that response is not the result of just that one sense organ nor is it a result of the addition of separate sense qualities. As Merleau-Ponty says: "I perceive a thing because I have a field of existence and because each phenomenon, on its appearance, attracts towards that field the whole of my body as a system of perceptual powers."[19]

Dewey concludes the chapter on "Substance and Form" by again asserting that live creature and environment are moments of one process: to separate the live creature from environment is to perpetuate the fruitless distinction between form and content which, when translated into philosophical theory, effortlessly expands into the debate between traditional empiricism and idealism. Dewey has attempted to show in this chapter that any absolute distinction between form and content, sense and meaning, is arbitrary. Because the perception of the artist or viewer is an expressive act, involving a crystallization of the entire field of habitual meanings, there can be no real distinction between perceptual meanings, motor meanings, or intellectual meanings. In the dialectic of constituting-constituted, the entire live creature is active; neither sense nor meaning possesses any sort of primacy, since in the expressive act of perception both are correlative and contemporaneous. Aesthetic experience, as an intensification of the drama of habit, enhances our susceptibility to the solicitations of the world; as Dewey says: "Whatever path the work of art pursues, it, just because it is a full and intense experience, keeps alive the power to experience the common world in its fullness."[20]

In "The Natural History of Form," Dewey's purpose is to clarify the notions of form, rhythm, and resistance or tension. The title itself of the chapter is significant, for it makes clear that presence of form is the outcome of a process or ordered movement. In the same sense that quality is the outcome of qualification, form is the result of formation; through the interaction of self and world, perception forms or constitutes an integrated or unified perceptual experience. For this reason, then,

---

[19]*Phenomenology*, p. 318.
[20]*Art as Experience*, p. 133.

form is not found exclusively in objects labeled works of art. Wherever perception has not been blunted and perverted, there is an inevitable tendency to arrange events and objects with reference to the demands of complete and unified perception. Form is a character of every experience that is *an* experience.[21]

It seems clear that Dewey has in mind the constitutive nature of perception, the fact that the form of the object and the form (or configuration) of the field of habitual meanings are strictly correlative. This is why he says that "form is a character of every experience that is *an* experience." The experiencing-experienced dialectic of habit and object is the source of form; form is a character of experience and not merely objects because only through the interaction of the intentional act of perception and the intentional object perceived is the form of that object actualized.

Dewey's definition of form is significant more for its suggestiveness than for its precision. He defines form as *"the operation of forces that carry the experience of an event, object, scene, and situation to its own integral fulfillment."*[22] As a corollary to this definition, Dewey concludes that "the connection of form with substance is thus inherent, not imposed from without."[23] Dewey's use of "forces" is somewhat vague, but it seems clear that he is referring to the reciprocal determination of habit and object. Through the dialectic of habit and object, the experience develops and grows, finally to reach a fulfillment or consummation. Thus, when Dewey talks about the "means" which carry forward an experience, he appears to have in mind the interaction or dialectic of intentional act, founded upon pre-objective habit, and intentional object. Furthermore, once form is seen as an outcome of the formative or constitutive power of habit in interaction with an object, any distinction (other than a purely functional distinction) between form and the matter which is formed, reveals itself to be grossly arbitrary. To enter into the experience of man, matter must be formed, even if it is on the mechanical level of perceptual recognition. An object is matter or meaning to man because, through habit, it has been formed into matter; an object, when experienced, *is* formed matter. Neither form or

---

[21]*Ibid.*, p. 137.
[22]*Ibid.*
[23]*Ibid.*

matter is logically or psychologically privileged, since each is a condition of the other's existence.

It at first may seen surprising that Dewey specifies certain general conditions of form, especially in light of his reluctance to impose a priori conceptual schemes on the concrete experience of the aesthetic. However, when examined closely, it is evident that the "general conditions involved in the orderly development of any subject-matter," are intimately related to the functioning of habit. Dewey writes:

> There can be no movement toward a consummating close unless there is a progressive massing of values, a cumulative effect. This result cannot exist without consideration of the import of what has gone before. Moreover, to secure the needed continuity, the accumulated experience must be such as to create suspense and anticipation of resolution.[24]

Continuity, cumulation, conservation, tension and anticipation are, according to Dewey, formal conditions of aesthetic form. It is fairly obvious that these conditions are characteristics of the drama of habit. Through the functioning of pre-objective habit, the accumulated meanings of past experience are conserved and rendered continuous with present experience. Also, habit "creates an unconscious expectation. It forms a certain outlook."[25] As habits are reformed into new configurations, there is suspense and anticipation as the consummation is dimly prefigured in the forming and reforming configurations of habits. There can be little doubt that the "formal conditions of esthetic form" are derived from the drama of habit.

Although Dewey considers it at greater length later in the chapter, it is noteworthy that he considers resistance to be of special importance. He remarks that "without internal tension there would be a fluid rush to a straightaway mark; there would be nothing that could be called development and fulfillment."[26] Unless the field of habitual meanings is sufficiently tensed, it will not provide sufficient resistance to the perceived object. In that case, the object will be assimilated by an isolated habit, with the result that there is no effect upon the general field of habitual meanings. In order for the artist or viewer to per-

[24]Ibid.
[25]Dewey, Human Nature, p. 75.
[26]Dewey, Art as Experience, p. 138.

ceive aesthetically, "he must remake his past experiences so that they can enter integrally into a new pattern."[27] Unless there is at least some reconstruction or reorganization of the pattern or configuration of the pre-objective field of habitual meanings, there is no drama of habit but merely a case of mechanical assimilation. Without the abrasion of habits and the resultant tension, there could be no aesthetic fulfillment or consummation, since the very basis and substance of fulfillment would be missing.

Dewey next inquires into "those formal conditions of artistic form that are rooted in the world itself." The basis of all form, he says, is interaction of self and world. "Interaction of environment with organism is the source, direct or indirect, of all experience and from the environment come those checks, resistances, furtherances, equilibria, which, when they meet with the energies of the organism in appropriate ways, constitute form."[28] This interaction of self and world is not a case of two separate, independent actions "interacting" with each other. Self and world constitute a single rhythm, although in any particular situation the initial solicitation may proceed from the self or the environment. The rhythm characterizing the dialectic of intentional act and intentional object is no less natural a rhythm of nature than the ebb and flow of tides or the systole and diastole of the flow of blood.

The essential point that Dewey is attempting to make in connection with rhythm is that "underneath the rhythm of every art and every work of art there lies, as a substratum in the depths of the subconsciousness, the basic pattern of the relations of the live creature to his environment."[29] In this statement, Dewey is referring to the two outstanding features of habit: its intentionality and its pre-objective nature. Habits embody the "achievements and victories" of the organism in its attempt to integrate itself with the environment in more satisfying ways. Habits are the record of past experiences and the soil from which future experiences will grow. Pre-objective habit is man's original openness or access to the world; it is the substratum upon which the compenetration of self and world is founded.

The "basic pattern" or general configuration of habits, which is a record and reflection of the "relations of the live creature to his en-

[27]*Ibid.*
[28]*Ibid.*, p. 147.
[29]*Ibid.*, p. 150.

vironment," is, according to Dewey, subconscious. Dewey always had been quite reluctant to ascribe a subconscious or unconscious status or source to experiences, because these concepts were so widely misused and misunderstood. Nevertheless, it was Dewey's belief that "because intellectual crimes have been committed in the name of the subconscious is no reason for refusing to admit that what is not explicitly present makes up a vastly greater part of experience than does the conscious field to which thinkers have so devoted themselves."[30] The subconscious substratum of habitual meanings is the horizon or context of taken for granted meanings which gives the objects of focal consciousness their "sense" as well as signification.

This substratum or field of pre-objective meanings is, when involved in an aesthetic experience, characterized by tension and resisting energies. This aspect of rhythm, variations in intensity, is a matter of some concern to Dewey because it is so intimately related to the functioning of habits. The integration of habits which occurs during an aesthetic experience comes as the consummation of the tensed dialectic of self and world. In response or answer to some solicitation of an object, the field of habitual meanings becomes tensed; the object is not figure nor is it background. As the expressive act of attention proceeds to develop the figure of the object, habits are reorganized into different configurations; there is tension and resistance as the energies of each habit are coordinated with those of other habits. Dewey writes:

> There must be energies resisting each other. Each gains intensity for a certain period, but thereby compresses some opposed energy until the latter can overcome the other which has been relaxing itself as it extends. The operation is reversed, not necessarily in equal periods of time but in some ratio that is felt as orderly.[31]

This process continues until the constituted object has emerged as figure against the background or context of taken for granted meanings.

It must not be forgotten that the field of habitual meanings does not become tensed in isolation from an intentional object. Thus, whether the intentional object is a horse or an idea of a horse, the field of ha-

---

[30]Dewey, *Experience and Nature*, 1st ed., p. 7.
[31]Dewey, *Art as Experience*, p. 155.

bitual meanings becomes tensed in interaction with the intentional object. This is merely a way of saying that habit and object are correlative; they are moments of a single rhythm or situation. Unless there is an interaction of constituting act and constituted object, there is no mutual solicitation. Hence, regardless of whether the initial solicitation comes from habit or object, unless the field of habitual meanings becomes tensed and remains so during its interaction with an intentional object, there is no situation and hence, no form, no rhythm, and no expression. Dewey says:

> There are multitudes of ways, varying between poles of tepid apathy and rough impatience, in which energy once aroused, fails to move in an ordered relation of accumulation, opposition, suspense and pause, toward final consummation of an experience. The latter is then inchoate, mechanical, or loose and diffuse. Such cases define by contrast, the nature of rhythm.[32]

Dewey is saying here that the habits of the organism must maintain a minimum level of tension or else there is "tepid apathy" and thus no situation since one's habits do not provide sufficient resistance in order for an object to emerge as figure. Instead, the object is immediately assimilated by an isolated habit or configuration of habits and therefore becomes ground before it ever was figure. In such a case, there is "too great openness of certain channels due to habits having become blind routines—when activity takes the form sometimes identified exclusively with 'practical' doing."[33] Because the field of habitual meanings is not sufficiently tensed, habits exist as isolated, discrete "channels" instead of as a web or matrix of interwoven meanings.

Similarly, when there is "rough impatience," no conservation or ordering of energies through reorganization of habits, there is mere expulsion and not expression. In this case, the field of habitual meanings is quite tensed, but there is no reorganization or reconstruction of meanings; the tension is simply "let loose on the environment in direct overt action."[34] Once again, no situation is constituted because there is no

---

[32]*Ibid.*, p. 157.
[33]*Ibid.*
[34]*Ibid.*, p. 156,

formative activity on the part of habits. Energy is released but not formed or expressed.

Dewey's conception of tension, resistance, and opposition has a profound implication with respect to his fundamental notion of interaction. He says that "polarity, or opposition of energies, is everywhere necessary to the definition, the delimitation, that resolves an otherwise uniform mass and expanse into individual forms."[35] Self and world are moments or aspects of a single system or single rhythm. This does not mean, however, that self and world are isomorphic with respect to energies simply because their energies are continuous. Except in cases of illness, there is an irreducible tension between the self and world. For this reason, experience is not homogeneous; there are beginnings and endings of experiences because the organism is both part of and apart from the environment. The organic interaction, or what Dewey in *Knowing and the Known*[36] called transaction, between self and environment, would be inconceivable unless there was sufficient tension between self and world so that their polar energies could form configurations and structures whereby what would otherwise be "uniform mass and expanse" is transformed into "individual forms."

At first, it may be difficult to imagine how it is that self and world are distinct yet continuous. It must be remembered, however, that Dewey's notion of interaction implies the concept of a *field*. He says that "wherever there is an event, there is interaction, and interaction entails the conception of a field."[37] Self and world are aspects or moments of a single field of existence. This field is a configuration or Gestalt which includes self and world as aspects of a "single tension," a single field of existence. The self is not the world nor is the world the self; yet, as Kwant says:

> The boundaries between me and the world, drawn by objective thought, fall away for anyone who recognizes the true character of intentionality. My seeing and hearing do not take place within the limits of my skin but in the field of my existence, in the world.[38]

[35]*Ibid.*, p. 157.
[36]John Dewey and Arthur F. Bentley, *Knowing and the Known* (Boston: Beacon Press, 1949), see pages 103-43.
[37]"A Naturalistic Theory of Sense Perception," *Philosophy and Civilization* (New York: Minton, Balch and Company, 1931), p. 198.
[38]*The Phenomenological Philosophy of Merleau-Ponty*, p. 67.

Self and world imply each other, but the self is not identical with the world, nor is the world identical with the self. Self and world are separated and joined by the "single tension" which is my field of existence, my world.

If self and world were not aspects of a "single tension," if they were identical in some sense, there could be no new rhythms established between them. Dewey says that one of the "objective modifications" effected by the formative arts (song, drama, music, and dance) is that "there is a direct lowering of tension between man and the world. Man finds himself more at home since he is in a world that he participated in making."[39] In such a case, man "becomes habituated and relatively at ease." This lowering of tension, however, potentially has inimical effects, because things may be made too smooth with the result that "there is not enough irregularity to create demand for a new manifestation and opportunity for a new rhythm."[40] New rhythms are born out of the tensed interaction of habitual self and world. Without a field of habitual meanings, there could be no field, no "single tension" whereby self and world mutually and reciprocally determine each other. As Merleau-Ponty says: "It is an inner necessity for the most integrated existence to provide itself with an habitual body."[41]

In "The Natural History of Form" Dewey makes repeated references to "energy" and "interaction of energies." The "inward energy" of the organism, embodied in it as habits, interact with the energies of the environment, whether in the form of finished art objects, in the case of the viewer, or works in the process of being created, in the case of the artist. From the standpoint of the organism, this "interaction of energies" is expressive; habitual meanings, based upon their constitutive or formative capacities, form the raw materials of words, paint, or clay, into an expressive object. In turn, the habitual meanings of the organism undergo change and transformation as they respond to the solicitation of the developing form. Energies are thus in opposition as the intentionality of habit insures the centrifugal and centripetal movement of *Sinngebung*. This opposition of energies is fundamentally dramatic; the reciprocal accommodation of self and world is fraught with suspense, uncertainty, and ambiguity. The "single tension" which sep-

[39]Dewey, *Art as Experience*, pp. 158-59.
[40]*Ibid.*, p. 159.
[41]*Phenomenology*, p. 87.

arates and joins self and world may be either too little or too great in a particular situation. Too little tension results in "tepid apathy"; the result of too much tension is violent discharge or release. In neither case, is there an adequate organization of energies.

Dewey begins the chapter on "The Organization of Energies" with a reaffirmation of the importance of pre-objective intentionality. He writes:

> Nothing enters experience bald and unaccompanied, whether it be a seemingly formless happening, a theme intellectually systematized, or an object elaborated with every living care of united thought and emotion. Its very entrance is the beginning of a complex interaction; upon the nature of this interaction depends the character of the thing as finally experienced. When the structure of the object is such that its force interacts happily (but not easily) with the energies that issue from the experience itself; when their mutual affinities and antagonisms work together to bring about a substance that develops cumulatively and surely (but not too steadily) toward a fulfilling of impulsions and tensions, then indeed there is a work of art.[42]

This passage provides a good example of the central importance of pre-reflective, pre-conscious intentionality in Dewey's philosophy of experience, aesthetic and nonaesthetic.

It is clearly implied in the passage that "things" may enter experience on a level of awareness which is prior to any sort of explicit, deliberate, conscious reflection. This is consistent with Dewey's belief that

> unless there is something immediately and non-cognitively present in experience so that it is capable of being pointed to in subsequent reflection and in action which embodies the fruits of reflection, knowledge has neither subject-matter nor objective.[43]

Any experience, no matter whether it is aesthetic or nonaesthetic, has its roots in pre-objective habit. Through the interaction or dialectic of habit and environment a situation is constituted which is permeated with a pervasive quality. This quality is the "something" that Dewey

---

[42]Dewey, *Art as Experience*, p. 162.
[43]*Experience and Nature*, 1st ed., pp. 21-22.

mentions as being immediately and noncognitively present in all experience. "Nothing enters experience bald and unaccompanied" because
having an experience and being in an experience require the active
participation of the self in the form of its pre-objective habits. The
entrance of something into experience means that it has been taken
up by the dialectic or interaction of self and world as part of the reciprocal constitution of intentional act and intentional object. The manner
or way in which a phenomenon is first taken up by the interaction of
self and world is of great importance, for "upon the nature of this interaction depends the character of the thing as finally experienced."

Dewey here is developing the same point which he had concerned
himself with in "The Postulate of Immediate Empiricism." He says in
that essay that

> by our postulate, things are what they are experienced to be;
> and, unless knowing is the sole and only genuine mode of ex-
> periencing, it is fallacious to say that Reality is just and ex-
> clusively what it is or would be to an all-competent all-knower;
> or even that it *is,* relatively and piecemeal, what it is to a finite
> and partial knower.[44]

In this essay Dewey is attempting to establish the fact that "things"
enter experience in a variety of ways; knowing is but one mode of gaining access to the world of objects and events. In claiming that things
"are what they are experienced as," Dewey is laying a heavy burden
upon the functioning of habit, because it is through the interaction of
pre-reflective, preconscious habit and the world, that things are immediately experienced and *experienceable.* To experience something *as* this
or that, and to experience it immediately *as* this or that, is to take advantage of the acquired and funded meanings embodied in habits. If
the human organism were not possessed of certain kinds of habits, nothing would be immediately experienceable, because there would be no
organic context or horizon of meanings whereby the solicitation of the
object or thing could be met by a pre-reflective, pre-conscious solicitation of the organism. To be in the world, and to be in it in such a way
that objects and events are immediately experienced and experienceable in the manner that Dewey describes in "The Postulate of Imme-

---

[44]"Immediate Empiricism," pp. 228-29.

diate Empiricism," the human organism must be an habitual-being-in-the-world.

With respect to aesthetic experience, the nature of the initial, immediate solicitation of self and world profoundly affects the character of the experience as it is finally had by the organism. One reason for this is that the initial, immediate solicitation of habit and object is also a process of qualification; the pervasive quality constituted by the interaction of habit and object is the basis for the continuation of the experience. Without this pervasive quality, the experience loses its sense and direction. Another reason why the initial, immediate solicitation of self and world is critical concerns the nature of perception. Since perception is an interaction of habit and object, their initial interaction results in the formation of the initial pattern or configuration of habitual meanings. This initial organization of pre-objective meanings of course undergoes change and reorganization as the experience develops. Nevertheless, the original, initial solicitation continues to exert a definite influence over the course of the experience's movement and development. The reason for this is that later solicitations of habit and object embody the original solicitation: the solicitation following the initial one is a refinement which in turn is followed by another, and so on. Thus, although the field of habitual meanings might be organized quite differently from what it was when the initial solicitation occurred, its final organization (as existing during the consumation of an aesthetic experience) is what it is and not something else because it is a development of the initial solicitation which gave it a unique pervasive quality.

Dewey's discussion of organization is basically concerned with how the organized energies of the art product affect and are affected by the organized energies of the self. Dewey deals with a number of considerations relevant to the organization of the energies of the art product and the self. The first consideration, that concerning the importance of the initial solicitation, already has been discussed. The importance of the original solicitation cannot be exaggerated, for it is the first actualization of the energies of both object and act which, up until then, has been only potential. It is for this reason that Dewey distinguishes between the "art product" which is "physical and potential," and the *"work* of art" which is "active and experienced."[45]

---

[45]*Art as Experience,* p. 162.

The next consideration relevant to the developing organization of energies is that this process takes time. Dewey says that

> in no case can there be *perception of an object* except in a process developing in time. Mere excitations, yes; but not an object perceived, instead of just recognized as one of a familiar kind.[46]

When the field of habitual meanings is involved in an aesthetic experience, there is reorganization of habits. This reorganization involves tension and resistance between the habits themselves and the habits and object. In order for there to be a consummation of this tension, there must be development and elaboration of the initial solicitation. This carrying forward of the original interaction takes time. The initial solicitation, unless extended and refined by further solicitations, is not a case of perception but rather of recognition. Although recognition serves many valuable functions in the course of the individual's affairs, it makes no sense to speak of an aesthetic recognition. All cases of aesthetic perception, and many cases of non-aesthetic perception, are processes which require time for their occurrence and, in aesthetic perception, their completion.

A third consideration relevant to the organization of energies, and perhaps the heart of the matter, is that, in the context of aesthetic experience, the energies of the work of art and those of the self are correlative. Dewey puts it precisely when he says that "perception and *its* object are built up and completed in one and the same continuing operation."[47] Dewey's phenomenological tendency is unmistakable here; intentional act and intentional object are moments of a "single tension." Through the functioning of pre-objective habit, perception becomes an expressive act whereby the perceiving and the perceived are reciprocally determinative. It is for this reason that Dewey speaks of the "object-of-perception,"[48] which is his way of emphasizing both the inseparability and reciprocity of act and object.

Dewey gives a detailed analysis of a painting which serves rather nicely to illustrate the points he has been trying to make with respect to the organization of energies. He writes:

---

[46]*Ibid.*, p. 175.
[47]*Ibid.*, p. 177.
[48]*Ibid.*

In looking at this particular object I have in mind, attention
is first caught by the objects in which masses point upward:
the first impression is that of movement from below to above.
This statement does not mean that the spectator is explicitly
conscious of vertically direct rhythms, but that, if he stops to
analyze, he finds that the first and dominant impression is determined by patterns so constituted by rhythms. Meantime
the eye is also moving across the picture though the interest
remains in patterns that rise. Then there is a halt, an arrest, a
punctuating pause as vision comes in the opposite lower
corner upon a definite mass that instead of fitting into the
vertical patterns transfers attention to the weight of horizontally
disposed masses. Were the picture badly composed, the variation would operate as a disturbing interruption, a break in
experience instead of as a re-direction of interest and attention, thus expanding the significance of the object. As it is,
the close of one phase of order gives a new set to expectancy
and this is fulfilled as vision travels back, by a series of colored
areas dominantly horizontal in character. Then, as that phase
of perception completes itself, attention is drawn to the ordered
variation in color characteristic of these masses. Then as attention is redirected to the vertical patterns—at the point from
which we set out—we miss the design constituted by color
variation and find attention directed toward spatial intervals
determined by a series of receding and intertwined planes. The
impression of depth, implicit of course, in perception from the
first is made explicit by this particular rhythmic order.[49]

It is significant that Dewey's analysis of the painting should proceed
by an account of the sequence or order of various acts of attention.
Dewey conceives of "attention" in almost exactly the same fashion as
Merleau-Ponty, who, says Langan, considered the act of attention to
be "the most basic intentional initiative a subject can take in order to
fill up the horizons offered to him and thus to provide himself with a
perceptual object."[50]

Merleau-Ponty develops his own theory of attention by first considering the shortcomings of the idealist (or what he calls intellectualist)
and empiricist theories. According to Merleau-Ponty:

---

[49]*Ibid.*, pp. 173-74.
[50]*Merleau-Ponty's Critique of Reason*, p. 40.

Where empiricism was deficient was in any internal connection between the object and the act which it triggers off. What intellectualism lacks is contingency in the occasions of thought. In the first case consciousness is too poor, in the second too rich for any phenomenon to appeal compellingly to it. Empiricism cannot see that we need to know what we are looking for, otherwise we would not be looking for it, and intellectualism fails to see that we need to be ignorant of what we are looking for, or equally again we should not be searching. They are in agreement in that neither can grasp consciousness *in the act of learning,* and that neither attaches due importance to that circumscribed ignorance, that still "empty" but already determinate intention which is attention itself.[51]

Both theories, then, see attention as a "general and formal activity" which "creates nothing."

In opposition to these theories, Merleau-Ponty conceives of attention as a constitutive, creative act. Attention is an expressive act; indeed, it is the most basic and fundamental expressive act since it is the ground for all other acts of expression. "The first operation of attention is, . . ." according to Merleau-Ponty, "to create for itself a *field,* either perceptual or mental, which can be 'surveyed' (*überschauen*), in which movements of the exploratory organ or elaborations of thought are possible. . . ."[52] The act of attention, in interaction with an object, creates (in the sense of reforming or restructuring) a field of meanings, a field where general horizons are gradually transformed into figures. For this reason, paying attention is not merely the elucidation of pre-existing data; it is, contrary to common belief, the active creation or constitution of phenomena as a result of the mutual solicitation of habit and object. Merleau-Ponty concludes that "attention is neither association of images, nor the return to itself of thought already in control of its objects, but the active constitution of a new object which makes explicit and articulate what was until then presented as no more than an indeterminate horizon."[53]

In Dewey's account of the acts of attention required to transform an art product into a *work* of art, there is little doubt that he is pursuing

---

[51]*Phenomenology,* p. 28.
[52]*Ibid.,* p. 29.
[53]*Ibid.,* p. 30.

a phenomenological course, one quite similar to Merleau-Ponty's. The original attentive act, the original solicitation, begins to crystallize the field of habitual meanings into a certain pattern or configuration. Meanings which had existed as context or horizon are now brought into increasingly sharp focus; meanings which had been focal now recede into the background. Dewey places great emphasis upon the first act of attention because it establishes the initial, preliminary configurations of the field of habitual meanings. Thus, although no act of attention is in any sense "irredeemable," i.e., cannot be followed by other attentive acts which change the configuration of habits achieved by the initial attentive act, the original solicitation *is* the first moment of a developing process, and as such, is the point of departure for later attentive acts. Because the solicitations which constitute an experience are not merely additive but cumulative, the original attentive act is, in a certain sense, present in the final or consummating attentive act.

Dewey makes it quite clear in his account of the attentive acts which build up a "pictorial perception," that this process takes time. The reorganization of the field of habitual meanings which occurs when horizons are transformed into figures and vice versa, is not an event of that instant. The mutual accommodation of habit and object may require a relatively short period of time for its completion, or it may involve an indefinitely long period of time before a consummatory solicitation occurs. In either case, it is apparent that attention involves time, and to speak of an act of attending which occurs instantly is not to speak of attending, but instead is to describe an act of noticing. In perceiving certain qualities of a painting, the viewer does not merely notice them, he attends to them, implying as this does, an intensification or concentration of energies which are diffuse and relatively unordered in the act of noticing.

Langan says that the perceived object "presents itself as still indeterminate possibility; it motivates the consciousness to take up what is still only ambiguous; with the help of the generalized resources of his sedimented experience of the world, the subject is able to determine the amorphous given into his object."[54] In interaction with the environment, habits—our "sedimented experience of the world"—constitute the perceptual object. The initial act of attention achieves a

---

[54]*Merleau-Ponty's Critique of Reason,* p. 41.

broad, general configuration of the pre-objective field. Both act and object are at this point quite indeterminate; the constituting-constituted dialectic has not yet reached a reciprocal accommodation whereby the field of habitual meanings has achieved a determinate organization, nor has the perceived object. The act of attentive perception is an act of constitution or creation where neither act or object possesses any sort of logical primacy. Dewey sums it up quite well when he says that "esthetic perception . . . is a name for a full perception and its correlative, an object or event."[55]

A fourth point related to the organization of energies, one which Dewey has referred to repeatedly, is that of tension, intensity, and resistance. He says that "where energy is rendered tense by reciprocal oppositions, it unfolds in ordered extension."[56] When a perceived object does not offer sufficient resistance to one's habitual meanings, there is no reciprocal solicitation since the object is assimilated by one habit or a relatively isolated configuration of habits. Because the object has been almost immediately assimilated by a certain habit, the habitual body does not assume a questioning attitude toward the object, with the result that there is no situation constituted whereby both self and world are mutually determinative. In a similar fashion, unless the habitual body possesses at least some taken for granted meanings relevant to a certain event or object, it will not offer any resistance to the event or object. In that case, the response of the subject will be grossly inappropriate with respect to developing the solicitation of the object or event, or else there simply will not be a response.

In discussing Merleau-Ponty's notion of incarnated intentionality, Langan says that the "anticipatory structures of the corps propre are always actively reaching out, but in normal perception they encounter resistances, solicitations, points of data which call upon and can cooperate with all the active powers of the natural-sensing body and all the sedimentations of the cultural body to become configured as meaningfully as the perceiver can make them."[57] In "The Organization of Energies," Dewey has developed essentially the same point which Langan attributes to Merleau-Ponty. In the course of *Art as Experience*, however, Dewey has come to place an increasingly heavy and persistent

---

[55]*Art as Experience*, p. 177.
[56]*Ibid.*, p. 182.
[57]*Merleau-Ponty's Critique of Reason*, pp. 64-65.

emphasis on the role of intensity, tension, and resistance in aesthetic experience and perception. The reason for this is contained in Kaelin's statement that "the phenomenal field is created by the tension between the organism and its environment."[58] Everything which Dewey has written up until the ninth chapter has contributed to an elaboration and expansion of the implications contained in his phrase, "single tension." The field of habitual meanings is one pole of this tension; the intentional object is the other pole. Taken together, these poles form a "single tension." Merleau-Ponty refers to this "single tension" as the "phenomenal field." In view of the phenomenological direction in which Dewey's analysis of aesthetic experience has been moving, it is not surprising that in "The Common Substance of the Arts," he explicitly takes up the notions of field and horizon.

---

[58]*An Existentialist Aesthetic*, p. 228.

CHAPTER V

THE SUBSTANCE OF THE ARTS

It was Dewey's belief that all the arts shared three common characteristics. First, every experienced matter of a work of art is set in a context of some undefined pervasive quality. Furthermore, "every work of art has a particular medium by which, among other things, the qualitative pervasive whole is carried."[1] Finally, space and time are found in every matter of a work of art, and are experienced as qualities of the total situation or experience. Of the three characteristics, the first is clearly the most fundamental, since the others are derived from it. A brief summary of Dewey's discussion of the context of pervasive quality will provide a setting for considering the full implications of his conceptions of pervasive quality and context with respect to his understanding of habit.

Dewey asserts that "artist and perceiver alike begin with what may be called a total seizure, an inclusive qualitative whole not yet articulated, not distinguished into members."[2] Dewey's use of "seizure" is quite vivid, and serves to emphasize the dramatic quality of the "single tension" which joins and separates self and environment in an aesthetic experience. At this point in the development of the experience, neither the energies of the object nor those of the organism have been fully organized through their interaction or dialectic. As the experience develops, the pervasive quality of the "single tension" implicating self and world undergoes discrimination. Attention structures and organizes the original seizure into figure and ground, and it is this background which provides the "pervasive qualitative unity" of the situation or "single tension."

Although attention discriminates parts and generally structures the experience into more determinate aspects, there is always an "indefinite total setting," a "qualitative 'background,'" which gives the objects of

---

[1]Dewey, *Art as Experience*, p. 195.
[2]*Ibid.*, p. 191.

80

experience (objects of reflection, awareness, etc.) their sense. This field or horizon "moves as we move. We are never free from the sense of something that lies beyond."[3] It is for this reason that "however broad the field, it is still felt as not the whole; the margins shade into that indefinite expanse beyond which imagination calls the universe."[4]

In support of his claims for the "undefined pervasive quality of an experience," Dewey points out that without this pervasive quality we would have no "sense of things as belonging or not belonging, of relevancy, a sense which is immediate." This sense of relevancy certainly is not a product of deliberate reflection, "for unless the sense were immediate we should have no guide to our reflection."[5] Dewey considers this context of pervasive quality so important that he says

> it is the essence of sanity. For the mad, the insane, thing to us is that which is torn from the common context and which stands alone and isolated, as anything must which occurs in a world totally different from ours.[6]

The "undefined pervasive quality of an experience" provides the implicit, non-cognitive, non-reflective context from which the explicit texts of consciousness are developed. In short, "without an indeterminate and undetermined setting, the material of any experience is incoherent."[7]

Both Dewey and Merleau-Ponty are in agreement that the indeterminate, the vague and ambiguous, are not incidental features of experience. As Merleau-Ponty says: "We must recognize the indeterminate as a positive phenomenon. It is in this atmosphere that quality arises."[8] Dewey was concerned with the indeterminate in two somewhat different senses. His theory of inquiry was a method of rendering indeterminate *situations* determinate or settled. In this case, the field of habitual meanings is indeterminate, i.e., lacking organization and configuration with respect to the solicitation of the objective circumstances. Through reflection, the field is reorganized and reconstructed in accordance with the demands of the solicitation of the circumstances with which the self interacts.

---

[3]*Ibid.*, p. 193.
[4]*Ibid.*, p. 194.
[5]*Ibid.*
[6]*Ibid.*, pp. 194-95.
[7]*Ibid.*, p. 195.
[8]*Phenomenology*, p. 6.

Dewey is concerned with, however, a sense of indeterminateness which is more general and basic than the sense in which it functions as a stage in the logical reconstruction of a problematic situation. This second sense is its ontological meaning. This use of indeterminate derives from the fact that the interaction of self and world, certainly Dewey's most fundamental conception, implies the notion of an *indeterminate field*. It will be remembered that Dewey stated that interaction "entails" the conception of a field.[9] The "single tension" of which self and world are moments or aspects, is a field of experience. Schrag comments that "experience, in its lived concreteness, is the act of experiencing figures (objects, events, situations, persons, moods, chimeras, hallucinations) not in isolation but contextualized within both determinate and indeterminate backgrounds."[10] Thus, the indeterminate and ambiguous are positive phenomena because they function as contexts for the texts of thematic consciousness. A closer examination will reveal the relationship between indeterminateness, quality, context, and habit in Dewey's ontology of experience.

When Dewey speaks of context he usually has in mind "that context of noncognitive but experienced subject-matter which gives what is *known* its import,"[11] as well as the circumstances or conditions of a particular situation, or what he sometimes simply calls "background."[12] With respect to background, Dewey means the spatial-temporal context of a particular situation.[13] It appears that by "context of noncognitive but experienced subject-matter" Dewey is referring to the functioning of pre-reflective, precognitive habits. Habitual meanings are the basis of that context which gives all conscious experiences their sense and import. These meanings are not objects of deliberate, conscious attention; yet, they are "in" the experience as much as the objects of critical reflection. Context and text are reciprocal and correlative; the text or focus of consciousness crystallizes the indeterminate or unordered meanings of the context into new configurations. The context of organic

---

[9]See above, p. 69.
[10]Schrag, *Experience and Being*, p. 18.
[11]*Experience and Nature*, 2nd ed., p. 22.
[12]See "Context and Thought" in *John Dewey on Experience, Nature, and Freedom* for his analysis of "background."
[13]See Schrag's chapter on "The Temporality and Spatiality of Experience" in his *Experience and Being* for a conception of time and space very similar to Dewey's.

habitual meanings provides the text of consciousness with its sense and direction; without the context of taken for granted meanings, there could be no text of consciousness since it would lack any sort of history, the history which is embodied in organic habits.

Dewey uses the example of writing to illustrate the relationship of text and context. He says:

> The word which I have just written is momentarily focal; around it there shade off into vagueness my typewriter, the desk, the room, the building, the campus, the town, and so on. *In* the experience, and in it in such a way as to *qualify* even what is shiningly apparent, are all the physical features of the environment extending out into space no one can say how far, and all the habits and interests extending backward and forward in time, of the organism which uses the typewriter and which notes the written form of the word only as temporary focus in a vast and changing scene.

Habitual meanings are in the experience not as texts of focal consciousness, but as meanings "lived" or "had." Because this context of pre-reflective, pre-conscious "lived" meanings (as opposed to known meanings) is a trait of every experience, Dewey concludes that consciousness "is only a very small and shifting portion of experience."[14]

It is noteworthy that in the passage cited, Dewey makes it unmistakably clear that habits, in interaction with the environment, *qualify* the texts of consciousness with a pervasive quality. The context of pre-objective habitual meanings is the basis of the "undefined pervasive quality of an experience." Without a context of habitual meanings, attention could not develop the solicitations of an object or event because there would be no pervasive quality to guide its movement and direction. Habits are the basis for the appearance of phenomena in experience, and because they qualify the experience with a pervasive quality, they are the basis for the development of an experience from its pre-objective roots to its later formulation in terms of determinate objects and distinctions.

However, the context of habitual meanings contributes to the development of an experience not only because it is the source of phenomena, "the layer of living experience through which other people

---

[14]"Introduction," *Essays in Experimental Logic*, p. 6.

and things are first given to us,"[15] nor because it qualifies the texts of consciousness with a pervasive quality. The meanings which are contextual are continuous with meanings which at the moment are text. In other words, habitual meanings provide the tools or instruments whereby focal consciousness transforms an indeterminate meaning into a distinct idea. Dewey's example of himself writing makes this apparent. Unless Dewey possessed certain sorts of habits—linguistic, intellectual, motor, etc.—he would not have the means to realize his conscious intentions or pre-objective intentions. In such a case, the texts of consciousness lack the instruments (habits) necessary for their development and elaboration. Unless the subject possesses relevant habits, the texts of consciousness will not be contextualized, i.e., incorporated within the configuration of pre-objective meanings. Dewey says that "the scope and content of the focused apparency have immediate dynamic connections with portions of experience not at the time obvious."[16] Without the presence of "immediate dynamic connections" between text and context, both become impoverished and incapable of growth and elaboration.

What, then, is the relationship between the indeterminate qualitative background and aesthetic experience? In view of the heavy emphasis Dewey has placed upon the intensification achieved by aesthetic experience, it is not surprising that his response to this query is formulated in terms of intensity. He says that "this sense of the including whole implicit in ordinary experiences is rendered intense within the frame of a painting or poem."[17] He later asserts that

> a work of art elicits and accentuates this quality of being a whole and of belonging to the larger all-inclusive, whole which is the universe in which we live. This fact, I think, is the explanation of that feeling of exquisite intelligibility and clarity we have in the presence of an object that is experienced with esthetic intensity.[18]

What Dewey seems to be saying is that in aesthetic experience, the "single tension" which joins self and world is purified, concentrated,

[15]Merleau-Ponty, *Phenomenology*, p. 57.
[16]"Introduction," *Essays in Experimental Logic*, p. 6.
[17]*Art as Experience*, p. 194.
[18]*Ibid.*, p. 195.

and intensified. Now this "single tension," or in Merleau-Pont's terms, "phenomenal field," is characterized in an aesthetic experience by the active participation of habitual self (intentional act) and work of art (intentional object). Consequently, an aesthetic intensification of the "single tension" of self-world implies an intensification of each of these aspects of the phenomenal field. The expressive object is, presumably, an organization of energies which embodies the ordered, intense energies of the artist's creative experience. The viewer's field of habitual meanings, when solicited by the work of art, is also intensified, with the result that dimensions and depths of the self are implicated in the aesthetic situation which normally are only latent and potential in ordinary experience.

Thus, through the intensification of the intentionality of habit achieved in aesthetic experience, self and world come to constitute a "whole" in a much more purified and concentrated manner than in normal or ordinary experience. The interaction or dialectic of habit and object in aesthetic experience is a dramatic intensification of man's fundamental condition: his being-in-the-world. Man's being and the world form a single system, a "single tension." Because man is related to the world intentionally and hence internally, the world is as much in us as we are in the world. Through our pre-objective habits, we carry the structures of the world with us, since habits are organic organizations of organism and environment. Dewey summarizes beautifully the sense of wholeness of self and world achieved by aesthetic experience when he writes that "we are citizens of this vast world beyond ourselves, and any intense realization of its presence with and in us brings a peculiarly satisfying sense of unity in itself and with ourselves."[19]

What is it, however, that accounts for that "undefined pervasive quality of an experience," and particularly, that "sense of something that lies beyond," a "sense of an enveloping undefined whole"? What Dewey seems to be suggesting by saying that "there is a bounding horizon," one "which moves as we move,"[20] is that the context of pre-objective habitual meanings is never exhausted, i.e., no matter how extensively the field of habitual meanings is involved in a situation, there are always meanings which remain contextual and non-thematic. Thus, if con-

---

[19]*Ibid.*
[20]*Ibid.*, p. 193.

sciousness is conceived of as a field of meanings ranging from those meanings which are focal objects, or as Dewey says, "objects of a cognitive regard, themes of an intellectual gesture,"[21] to those habitual meanings which provide the context of the texts of consciousness, it is apparent that there still are habitual meanings which are not actively involved in that particular solicitation. Nevertheless, these relatively passive habits are not unrelated to those habits active in the present interaction, hence, there is always a "sense of something that lies beyond" because there are always habits which are partially implicated in the constitution of a solicitation, but which are not as active as those habits which are most immediately involved in the present experience. Naturally, habits which are active in one experience, providing the active context of the text of consciousness, may in another experience assume a less active role. Thus, there is always something left over when the field of habitual meanings is solicited by an object; there is always an "indeterminate and undetermined" portion of the field which functions as a "bounding horizon" for the text and context of consciousness.

When Dewey's discussion of the "qualitative pervasive whole" is carefully examined, there is a growing sense that Dewey is driving at something which is not readily apparent, or which at least is left implicit. Calvin O. Schrag's consideration of the philosophical conception of the concrete provides a setting for examining Dewey's notion of "qualitative pervasive whole" in a more comprehensive and penetrating manner. Referring to "concrete," Schrag writes:

The word itself is of Latin origin, derived from the infinite *concrescere,* meaning simply "to grow together." Although etymology never answers any philosophical problems, it may be a helpful guide in placing us on the proper path. Speaking of *the concrete* is already a grammatical abstraction. What is at issue is the *event of concretion,* the process in which the constituents of experience in some sense mix and mingle and conspire as an appearance or a phenomenon. We are thus able to see how the configurative and process character of experience . . . can properly be understood as the presentation of events of concretion. To speak of the concrete is to articulate the presence of the experiential field as a process in which ex-

[21]"Introduction," *Essays in Experimental Logic,* p. 4.

periencer, figure, and background conspire or grow together. The dynamic phenomenal field is determined by concreteness.[22]

According to Schrag, to fully understand in what sense the concrete is an event of "concretion," it must first be understood in what sense experience may be said to be "immediate." He says that

> the immediate, as applied to experience, has to do with that which is *directly* presented, without the intervention of a "go-between" or a "by virtue of which. . . ." The deliverance of the concrete is direct rather than circuitous, following neither the lure of abstracted sense-data nor the vapor of mediating concepts. Concreteness is delivered in its immediacy through a response to the invitation, "Look and see."[23]

When Dewey's conception of "immediately experienced" "pervasive quality" is examined against the background of Schrag's discussion, it becomes evident that the notion of concretion is extremely helpful in understanding some of the less obvious features of Dewey's notion of qualitative immediacy and its connection with habit.

Even a superficial reading of Dewey will reveal the enormous philosophical significance he attributed to concrete experience.[24] Thus, in "The Postulate of Immediate Empiricism," he takes the example of the experience of a startling noise to illustrate the distinction between what something is *known as* and what something is concretely *experienced as*. The noise as experienced is fearful: "that *is what* it is experienced as being." Its appearance in experience, in other words, is as a fearsome noise and, according to Dewey, "it *really* is, not merely phenomenally or subjectively so."[25] When the noise is experienced as a *known* thing, i.e., when it is inquired into, then it is discovered that there is no reason to be fearful, for it is found to be merely the tapping of a shade against the window. Dewey says the "experience has changed: that is, the thing experienced has changed—not that an unreality has given place to a reality, nor that some transcendental (unexperienced) Reality has

---

[22]*Experience and Being,* p. 33.

[23]*Ibid.,* p. 36.

[24]Dewey concludes the first chapter of *Experience and Nature* (1929) by saying: "If what is written in these pages has no other result than creating and promoting a respect for concrete human experience and its potentialities, I shall be content." p. 36.

[25]"Immediate Empiricism," p. 230.

changed, not that truth has changed, but just and only the concrete reality experienced has changed."[26] Schrag's conception of concretion helps to clarify what Dewey is saying. When the noise is concretely experienced as fearful, there is a particular concretion of the various constituents of the experience; these constituents "mix and mingle and conspire as an appearance or a phenomenon." Hence, the "concrete reality experienced" is the outcome or result of a particular concretion or "growing together" of the constituents of the experience. If the noise was rhythmical instead of sharp, distant instead of near, accompanied by other disturbances instead of alone, then it is likely there would have been a different concretion, i.e., a different "concrete reality experienced." It is also obvious that the habits of the organism affect the nature of the concretion. If one possesses certain kinds of perceptual, motor, and cognitive habits, a sharp, unexpected noise may be concretely experienced as fearsome. On the other hand, it is conceivable that one may be habituated to the occurrence of irregular, unexpected noises. In such a case, the noise concretely experienced will be qualitatively different from the noise experienced by someone with different habits. In other words, the experience is qualitatively different, and is experienced as such, because there is a different concretion of constituents.

Thus, Dewey is saying that immediate, concrete experience (or what he variously calls ordinary experience, primary experience, macroscopic experience, crude experience, noncognitive experience, nonreflectional experience, and experience which is "had") is always a matter of a "concrete qualitative thing or *that*."[27] Immediate, direct (in Schrag's sense of being free from the "vapor of mediating concepts"), concrete experience is always characterized by a pervasive quality. It previously has been stated that pervasive quality is the outcome of a process of qualification wherein habit and object cooperate or interact in constituting a pervasive quality which affects the entire situation. Schrag's notion of concretion helps to emphasize the sense in which it may be said that the pervasive quality of a situation is the result of the interaction, cooperation, or "growing together" of habit and object. Qualitative immediacy is derived from the concretion of habit and object; aesthetic experience is an intensification of this concretion through the overcoming of resistance.

[26] *Ibid.*
[27] *Ibid.*, p. 234.

When Dewey's philosophy of aesthetic experience is viewed against the background provided by Schrag's discussion of concretion, it is not surprising that in the first chapter of *Art as Experience* Dewey indicts existing theories of art because "they start from a ready-made compartmentalization, or from a conception of art that 'spiritualizes' it out of connection with the objects of concrete experience."[28] When Dewey says that art is a celebration of ordinary or concrete experience, he implicitly is saying that aesthetic experience is an intensification of the concretions of ordinary experience.

In "The Act of Expression," Dewey provides a clue to the way in which he understands concrete experience. He says that "immediacy and individuality, the traits that mark concrete existence, come from the present occasion; meaning, substance, content, from what is embedded in the self from the past."[29] It seems clear that Dewey is describing the concretion of the phenomenal field, the "growing together" of habitual (and hence, historical) self and world. This concretion of habit and object in a particular situation involves "an intimate union of the features of present existence with the values that past experiences have incorporated in personality."[30] Dewey's insistence that an expressive act necessarily involves a *fusion* of past, present, and future, is clearly his way of emphasizing the concretion which occurs when habit and object are reciprocally implicated in a particular situation. It may be said that a situation is a concretion of self and word, and of the field of time within which both are moments.

Every concretion of self and world results in a pervasive quality. This quality is immediately or directly felt, i.e., it is not the result of any sort of deliberate or critical reflection on the part of the subject. In this concretion of self and world, there is a concretion of the field of habitual meanings. In response to the solicitation of some object, the field becomes tensed: portions of it "grow together" to form new configurations. This concretion of the pre-objective field solicits a response from the object; in this way, the experienced object also undergoes a process of concretion as details or aspects of it are incorporated into an experienced whole. Thus, every situation within which self and world are moments of a "single tension," is qualitatively and concretely just

---

[28]*Art as Experience*, p. 11.
[29]*Ibid.*, p. 71.
[30]*Ibid.*

what it is and nothing else, because the concretion of constituents which form the situation is just what it is, a "that" as Dewey says, and nothing else.

Aesthetic experience is an intensification of this process of concretion. Even in ordinary experience the concretion of the field of habitual meanings, of the experienced object, and of self and world, does not occur in one uninterrupted sweep. As the constituents of an experience "mix and mingle and conspire as an appearance or a phenomenon," there is some tension and resistance as the centrifugal and centripetal powers of habit struggle to achieve a satisfactory configuration. However, in ordinary experience, concretions are partial; there is not a continuous and cumulative series of solicitations of habit and object whereby the field of habitual meanings and the phenomenal field reach a fulfilling or consummating configuration. Either the tension characterizing the pre-objective field is too little, in which case the concretion of constituents does not proceed far enough to reach an ordered consummation, or else there is too much tension with the result that the concretion is again truncated because this time there is mere release or expulsion instead of expression.

The notion of concretion is helpful in understanding certain other features of Dewey's aesthetic theory. Thus, he says that "in every experience, there is the pervading underlying qualitative whole that corresponds to and manifests the whole organization of activities which constitute the mysterious human frame."[31] Dewey's constant emphasis upon "wholeness" of the organism when involved in an aesthetic experience is his way of reinforcing the necessity of an intense concretion of the "activities which constitute the mysterious human frame," or, in Merleau-Ponty's terms, the habitual body. Without this concretion of the organism's habits, there can be no aesthetic experience. There need not be an actual reconstruction of the entire field of habitual meanings, but unless there is a continuous and cumulative concretion of the organism's perceptual, motor, and cognitive habits, the expression will lack the unity and integration which characterizes aesthetic expression.

Furthermore, the act of expression is a concretion of the field of

---

[31]*Ibid.*, p. 196.
[32]For examples of this in *Art as Experience* see pp. 60, 65, 71, and 98-99.

time. Dewey constantly emphasizes[32] that the meanings derived from prior experiences and those existing in the present experience are "fused in the fire of internal commotion." Dewey of course had already in the first chapter touched upon this sort of concretion when he said that "art celebrates with peculiar intensity the moments in which the past reenforces the present and in which the future is a quickening of what now is."[33] Discussing in what sense concretion is an immediate, direct event, Schrag gives support to Dewey's conception of the field of time. Schrag writes:

> To speak of the immediate is already to speak of time. The immediate is confronted in a *moment* of time. But this moment of time is not an abstracted instant of serial succession. It is a moment with fringes and a temporal background of past and future. The immediacy of the concrete is thus already a temporalized immediacy, a presence surrounded with retentions and protentions. There is no perception of the immediate in an instant, abstracted and cut off from the flow of the past through the present into the future. What is required for the elucidation of the immediacy of the given is a view of time other than that of mere serial succession in which past, present, and future are pulverized into discrete and granular units which succeed each other in an endless coming to be and passing away. The presence of immediacy is an *ecstatic* presence—a presence which stands out into a future and streches back into a past.[34]

Habits are our inherence in the field of time; through their functioning, there is a concretion of past, present, and future. Aesthetic experience is an intensification and purification of such concretion.

The concretion of self and world, that "single tension" wherein self and world are mutually and reciprocally determinative, is a characteristic of every normal experience. Aesthetic experience, it has been said, is an intensification, concentration, and purification of this concretion. In the course of the development of *Art as Experience,* Dewey has placed greater and greater emphasis upon the reciprocity of habit and object in an aesthetic experience. Having considered in "The Common Substance of the Arts" and "The Varied Substance of the Arts,"

---

[33]*Art as Experience,* p. 18.
[34]*Experience and Being,* p. 37.

the basis of a work of art's contribution to a particular concretion of self and work of art, Dewey is now prepared to examine the role of the habitual self in an aesthetic experience. A major assumption of Dewey's examination is that "no complete account of what is experienced . . . can be given until we know *how* it is experienced, or the mode of experiencing that enters into its formation."[35] Thus, Dewey concludes his analysis of the experiencing-experienced transaction involved in aesthetic experience by considering "the human contribution" to that dialectic, and it is in this consideration that Dewey's phenomenological tendencies reach their most articulate expression.

---

[35]"Conduct and Experience," *Philosophy and Civilization* (New York: Minton, Balch and Company, 1931), p. 261.

CHAPTER VI

THE HUMAN CONTRIBUTION

In his discussion of the contribution of the self to an aesthetic experience, Dewey makes it clear that self and world are reciprocally determinative. He says:

> Because every experience is constituted by interaction between "subject" and "object," between a self and its world, it is not itself merely physical nor merely mental, no matter how much one factor or the other predominates. The experiences that are emphatically called, because of the dominance of the internal contribution, "mental," have reference, direct or remote, to experiences of a more objective character; they are the products of discrimination, and hence can be understood only as we take into account the total normal experience in which both inner and outer factors are so incorporated that each has lost its special character.[1]

Any experience is, to some extent, a concretion of self and world; in an aesthetic experience this concretion is so complete that self and world become moments of a "single tension," aspects of a unified phenomenal field. Thus, even in the most ordinary, nonaesthetic experience, the relationship between self and world is never completely external. Dewey declares that "intrinsic connection of the self with the world through reciprocity of undergoing and doing; and the fact that all distinctions which analysis can introduce into the psychological factors are but different aspects and phases of a continuous, though varied, interaction of self and environment, are the two main considerations that will be brought to bear in the discussion that follows.[2]

When the relationship between self and world is viewed as an external and not intrinsic relationship, the phenomenon of "projection" appears almost defensible. According to this view, aesthetic qualities

---

[1] *Art as Experience*, p. 246.
[2] *Ibid.*, p. 247.

are projected by the mind into the art object. If the self and world were merely contingently related, it would not be unreasonable to think that an art object acts as a sort of "stimulus" which activates a response, i.e., the projection of qualities into it. Habitual self and world are not, however, separate systems of causality which somehow "interact" with one another. Habit and object are aspects of a single phenomenal field. When there is an intensified concretion of this field in an aesthetic experience, "organism and environment cooperate to institute an experience in which the two are so fully integrated that each disappears.[3] What Dewey is attempting to emphasize is that the habitual self, because it "is a force, not a transparency,"[4] and the world, form a "single tension" which is intensified and purified in an aesthetic experience.

When Dewey speaks of "the human contribution," he is referring to the contribution of the habitual self to the constitution of an experienced situation. Because of the intentionality of habits, the fact that they "are always *of, from, toward,* situations and things,"[5] "the human contribution" is never without a world. Man is a being-in-the-world because, as Merleau-Ponty says, "the human body, with its habits which weave round it a human environment, has running through it a movement toward the world itself."[6] Thus, "the human contribution" is a correlate of the contribution of the world; it is for this reason that knowledge of just extra-organic conditions "may account for a happening in the abstract but not for the concrete or experienced happening."[7] The experienced happening is a concretion of the contributions of the habitual self and those of the world. Any account of the experienced situation which fails to consider both aspects constituting the situation is incomplete and partial.

Dewey is particularly concerned to establish the worldliness of "the human contribution" because

> whenever the bond that binds the living creature to his environment is broken, there is nothing that holds together the various factors and phases of the self. Thought, emotion, sense, purpose, impulse fall apart, and are assigned to dif-

---

[3]*Ibid.,* p. 249.
[4]*Ibid.,* p. 246.
[5]Dewey, *Experience and Nature,* 2nd ed., p. 195.
[6]*Phenomenology,* p. 327.
[7]Dewey, *Experience and Nature,* 2nd ed., p. 195.

ferent compartments of our being. For their unity is found in the cooperative roles they play in active and receptive relations to the environment.[8]

Perceptual habits, motor habits, and cognitive habits even in ordinary, non-aesthetic experience, are marked by a minimal degree of integration, fusion, or concretion. This concretion of habitual meanings is a function of their intentionality, i.e., the fact that they are aspects of that "single tension" constituted by the interaction or dialectic of self and world. If it were not the case that "environing objects avail and counteravail,"[9] there would be no tension or resistance between the self and world. In that case, the field of habitual meaning would cease to exist as a field; lacking any sort of internal, intrinsic connection with the world, there would be no continuity of the tensed energies of the phenomenal field and the tensed energies of the field of habitual meanings. Without some degree of tension, the pre-objective field would lose its identity as an ordered field and become a mixture of discrete, isolated meanings. Thus, habits are in the world as much as they are in the organism since man himself is a being-in-the-world. The continuity of habitual self and world is a necessary and not contingent trait of existence.

Dewey never tires of reminding the reader that aesthetic experience "is marked by a greater inclusiveness of all psychological factors than occurs in ordinary experiences."[10] Consistent with this statement about the concretion of psychological factors is Dewey's belief that "motor and sensory structure form a single apparatus and effect a single function."[11] This belief is supported by Merleau-Ponty, who says:

> The analysis of motor habit as an extension of existence leads on, then, to an analysis of perceptual habit as the coming into possession of a world. Conversely, every perceptual habit is still a motor habit and here equally the process of grasping a meaning is performed by the body. When a child grows accustomed to distinguishing blue from red, it is observed that the habit cultivated in relation to these two colors helps with the rest.[12]

---

[8]*Art as Experience,* p. 252.
[9]*Ibid.,* p. 16.
[10]*Ibid.,* p. 254.
[11]*Ibid.,* p. 255.
[12]*Phenomenology,* p. 153.

In an aesthetic experience, there is a concretion not only of perceptual and motor habits, but of all organic habits. It is for this reason that in an aesthetic experience there is no distinction between perceptual sense and meaning; as Dewey says: "Art has the faculty of enhancing and concentrating this union of quality and meaning in a way which vivifies both."[13] Thus, aesthetic experience is an intensification of the concretion of habitual meanings, a concretion which is minimally present in ordinary experience but which in aesthetic experience is purified and concentrated.

Because "the human contribution" to an aesthetic experience is commonly considered to be effected through the "mind" of the subject, Dewey turns his attention to the concept of mind in order to clarify the sort of contribution which mind makes to an aesthetic experience. This involves Dewey in a discussion of the intentionality of mind and the structure of mind. With respect to the former consideration, Dewey is relatively brief, since he has already quite firmly established that the mind or self cannot be specified apart from, or independent of, the world, and similarly, the world cannot be specified independently from the way it is experienced *as* by an organism, i.e., its mode of appearance to the mind or self. Dewey summarizes his basic position with respect to the intentionality of mind by saying that mind "never denotes anything self-contained, isolated from the world of persons and things, but is always used with respect to situations, events, objects, persons and groups."[14] When mind is taken to be "primarily a verb,"[15] i.e., when it is viewed as certain "modes of action" in and upon the environment, then connection between mind and world can be recognized more easily as being intrinsic and inherent, necessary rather than contingent.

When mind is considered as "modes of action" there is another benefit in addition to the fact that its internal relationship to the world is made more apparent. This benefit is that the relationship between body and mind is seen to be necessary and not contingent; as Dewey says: "Every 'mind' that we are empirically acquainted with is found in connection with some organized body."[16] Dewey is made impatient by

---

[13]*Art as Experience,* p. 259.
[14]*Ibid.,* p. 263.
[15]*Ibid.*
[16]*Experience and Nature,* 2nd ed., p. 226.

the fact that "we have no word by which to name mind-body in a unified wholeness of operation,"[17] and simply assumes that when he talks about "mind" or "self" it is taken for granted that he is referring to the body-mind, the single reality of the physical and mental. Consequently, there is a sense in which mind is obviously "substantial." Dewey writes:

> Whenever anything is undergone in consequence of a doing, the self is modified. The modification extends beyond acquisition of greater facility and skill. Attitudes and interests are built up which embody in themselves some deposit of the meaning of things done and undergone. These funded and retained meanings become a part of the self.

In this sense, then, mind is substantial; it provides an active background "upon which every new contact with surroundings is projected."[18]

It is helpful here to remember that an attitude is, for Dewey, a "non-patent" form of habit.[19] An interest is "an unconscious but organic bias toward certain aspects and values of the complex and variegated universe in which we live."[20] Interests are founded upon habit. Without the existence of quite well-established habits, the interests typical of the "scientific mind," the "executive mind," the "artistic mind," and other kinds of "minds," would lack any sort of substance. There would be no context of taken for granted meanings whereby the texts of conscious interest and attention could derive sense and direction. Furthermore, unless interests are continuous with relevant habits, there will be little chance that the interests will grow and develop, since without a context of pre-objective habits, an interest lacks the tools or instruments for its own expansion and refinement.

When Dewey talks about different kinds of "minds,' he of course is touching upon the work he did in "The Interpretation of the Savage Mind."[21] In that essay he showed that the basis of the difference between the "mind" of the hunter and the "mind" of the farmer is understandable in terms of the different habits their occupations tended to develop. Dewey again takes up this matter of "minds" in *Human Na-*

---

[17]"Body and Mind," p. 302.
[18]Dewey, *Art as Experience*, p. 264.
[19]See above, p. 60.
[20]Dewey, *Art as Experience*, p. 95.
[21]See above, pp. 15-19.

ture and Conduct. In the chapter on "Habit and Intelligence," Dewey notes that the sailor is at home on the sea, the hunter in the forest, the scientist in the laboratory, the painter in the studio, and so on. These are, Dewey says, commonplaces, and "they mean nothing more or less than that habits formed in process of exercising biological aptitudes are the sole agents of observation, recollection, foresight and judgment: a mind or consciousness or soul in general which performs these operations is a myth."[22] The point which must be made with respect to Dewey's discussion of mind on pages 262-266 in *Art as Experience,* is that although he seems to identify "interest" and not habit as the basic structure of mind, it must be understood that for Dewey, when an interest ("always at work below the surface") reaches down into the deeper levels of selfhood, it is basically a configuration of certain habits.

Dewey makes this clear in his brief discussion of the importance of tradition to the artist. Tradition forms a large part of the background of experience which an artist brings to a certain situation. Dewey writes that

> each great tradition is itself an original habit of vision and of methods of ordering and conveying material. As this habit enters into native temperament and constitution it becomes an essential ingredient of the mind of an artist.[23]

When a painter has a substantial interest (in Dewey's sense of the word) in say, the relationship between space and "empty" space, certain, or all, of his "habits of vision" as well as other organic habits, are grouped into particular configurations. Thus, to say that a painter has an interest in space and "empty" space, one is in effect saying that the background of experience of the painter, his mind, is organized in a certain manner, and that it is likely he will attend to certain aspects of a situation rather than to others. His interest in a scene is a function of the habits which give it body and substance. Hence, habit and interest meet and become one on the level of pre-objective experience.

In page after page of *Art as Experience,* Dewey states that in an aesthetic experience, past, present, and future "fuse" or interpenetrate so thoroughly that they become one moment in the field of time. This

---

[22]*Human Nature,* p. 176.
[23]*Art as Experience,* p. 265.

concretion of the field of time is based on a field conception of mind and consciousness. Dewey writes:

> Mind is more than consciousness, because it is the abiding even though changing background of which consciousness is the foreground. Mind changes slowly through the joint tuition of interest and circumstance. Consciousness is always in rapid change, for it marks the place where the formed disposition and the immediate situation touch and interact. It is the continuous readjustment of self and the world in experience. "Consciousness" is the more acute and intense in the degree of the readjustments that are demanded, approaching the nil as the contact is frictionless and interaction fluid. It is turbid when meanings are undergoing reconstruction in an undetermined direction, and becomes clear as a decisive meaning emerges.[24]

Implicit in Dewey's field theory of mind and consciousness is a field theory of meaning, and it is this theory of meaning which is fundamental to his conception of aesthetic experience as an intensified concretion of the field of habitual meanings.

In the chapter on "Existence, Ideas and Consciousness" in *Experience and Nature,* Dewey says that there is a "continuum" or "spectrum" between the meanings of mind and the focal ideas of consciousness: "There is a contextual field between the latter and those meanings which determine the habitual direction of our conscious thoughts and supply the organs for their formation."[25] Dewey takes the notion of a "field" in a fairly literal sense, and for this reason he believes that words like "context," "background," and "fringe" suggest "something too external to meet the facts of the case." Habits of mind—meanings integrated in organic functions—constitute the taken for granted meanings of the organism. These habitual meanings influence behavior and experience in a more organically pervasive and suffusive manner than words like context, background, and fringe seem to suggest. Dewey's example of seeing and hearing a drama illustrate this point.

In order to understand and appreciate the present phase of a play, the meanings derived from the earlier portions of the play must be present in the perception now had. If we had to deliberately remem-

---

[24]*Ibid.,* pp. 265-66.
[25]*Experience and Nature,* 2nd ed., pp. 248-49.

ber them, our attention would be divided between the past and the present. This is not the case when present perception is aesthetic because "the purport of past affairs is present in the momentary cross-sectional idea in a way which is more intimate, direct and pervasive than the way of recall."[26] The present perception does not contain an act of recollection; the viewer has a "sense" of the meanings of previous action, and his present perception is a fulfillment of the meanings of previous action. The present perception is also anticipatory; it reaches into the future because it throws the meanings funded from previous action into suspense and uncertainty. Meanings acquired from past action are indeterminate, for as the action progresses they assume a different sense and direction. Dewey concludes that

> it is this double relationship of continuation, promotion, carrying forward, and of arrest deviation, need of supplementation, which defines that focalization of meanings which is consciousness, awareness, perception. Every case of consciousness is dramatic; drama is an enhancement of the conditions of consciousness.[27]

Because meanings exist in the form of a field, past, present, and future meanings are continuous and hence qualify each other. Our present perception incorporates into itself a "sense" of the past and of the future; these meanings are not arrived at through discrete acts of remembering or predicting. As Merleau-Ponty says:

> In every focusing movement my body unites present, past and future, it secretes time, or rather it becomes that location in nature where, for the first time, events, instead of pushing each other into the realm of being, project round the present a double horizon of past and future and acquire a historical orientation.[28]

In an aesthetic experience this "focusing" of the habitual body is intensified and concentrated.

It has been shown that habitual meaning affords the pre-objective context for the specification of thematic texts (ideas). The immediate,

---

[26]Ibid., p. 249.
[27]Ibid., p. 250.
[28]Phenomenology, pp. 239-40.

pervasive quality of a situation gives us its "sense"—its lived meaning. Dewey's field theory of meaning enabled him to treat the experience of having a "sense of" something as a philosophical matter. James, of course, was Dewey's teacher with respect to the pre-reflective and pre-conscious. Using single words like halo, fringe, penumbra, and feeling, as well as remarkable phrases like, "premonitory perspective views of schemes of thought not yet articulate,"[29] James constructed a phenomenology of lived meaning. Not surprisingly, then, James speaks of having a "sense of" something[30] to refer to the lived, pre-reflective level of experience. However, James seems not to have closed the circle of habit, sensed meaning, and the pre-reflective as tightly and carefully as Dewey. This may be due to James's failure to see habit as something more than the "precious conservative agent" of society. Thus, James wishes to make habit an "ally" by "living at ease" through the meaning funded in habit. To do this, *we must make automatic and habitual, as early as possible, as many useful actions as we can."*[31] James uncovered the drama of the pre-reflective, meanings lived or sensed, but overlooked the pre-reflective intentionality of habit.

To have a "sense of" something is to take advantage of the work done by the field of habitual meanings. This field achieves the pre-predicative unity or fusion of perception and reflection which enables the products, the sedimentations, of the latter to exist immediately in perceptual experience. Dewey states:

> Sense is distinct from feeling, for it has a recognized reference; it is the qualitative characteristic of something, not just a submerged unidentified quality or tone. Sense is also different from signification. The latter involves use of a quality as a sign or index of something else, as when the red of a light signifies danger, and the need of bringing a moving locomotive to a stop. The sense of a thing, on the other hand, is an immediate and immanent meaning; it is meaning which is itself felt or directly had. When we are baffled by perplexing conditions, and finally hit upon a clew, and everything falls into place, the whole thing suddenly, as we say, "makes sense." In such a situation, the clew has signification in virtue of being

---

[29]*The Principles of Psychology,* Vol. I (New York: Dover Publications, Inc., 1890), p. 253.
[30]*Ibid.,* pp. 253-54.
[31]*Ibid.,* p. 122.

an indication, a guide to interpretation. But the meaning of the *whole* situation as apprehended is sense.[32]

The aesthetic marks those moments of experience where one's capacity to "sense" is quickened and deepened. These moments "exhibit an integral union of sense quality and meaning in a single firm texture."[33]

Thus, one may experience a sense of vastness, of terror, a sense of what D. H. Lawrence calls "appleyness." Words and concepts may also be sensed. Dewey uses the example of "friend" and "enemy." These words, he says, "make immediate sense as well as have signification."[34] To know the meaning of a word is to know more than the rules for its use. To know a word, e.g., "friend" or "enemy," is to have at least partially transformed one's habits, the organic structures which pre-reflectively establish a world and a meaning for me. To have a sense of a word, then, involves more than the productive competencies of what Dewey calls the "linguistic apparatus." In summary, "the more intimate the alliance of vocal activity with the total organic disposition toward friends and enemies, the greater is the immediate sense of the words."[35]

When one experiences the "sense of" something, then, the distance between perception and reason, impulse and wisdom, is narrowed. The initial "sense of" something may be partial, confused, contradictory. If the experience moves toward aesthetic fulfillment, the ambiguity of this "sense" is not so much eliminated as developed into a lucidity which is tensely poised against the insistent "sense of something that lies beyond."[36] As our "sense of" something gains wider perspective and greater depth, our field of habitual meanings is composed and decomposed, until finally the invisible yields a lived meaning which has been not so much hidden as unrealized. The aesthetic is the realization and intensification of the drama of habit, a drama where the lucidity of reason is embodied in "emotionally charged sense,"[37] a lucidity, then, which is never a final synthesis.

Dewey's generalization that "every case of consciousness is dramatic; drama is an enhancement of the conditions of consciousness,"

---

[32]*Experience and Nature,* 2nd ed., p. 213.
[33]Dewey, *Art as Experience,* p. 259.
[34]*Experience and Nature,* 2nd ed., p. 238.
[35]*Ibid.,* pp. 238-39.
[36]*Art as Experience,* p. 193.
[37]*Ibid.,* p.33.

suggests that there is more in his example of viewing a drama than there initially appears to be. The most obvious meaning of Dewey's example is that the meanings of the play fuse and interpenetrate without the intervention of deliberate, critical thought. However, it is obvious that the meanings of the play are realized or actualized in interaction with the habitual meanings of the viewer. The meanings suggested by the play "make sense" to the viewer only as they are taken up and constituted by the habitual meanings of the perceiver. Thus, the crystallization or concretion of meanings effected by a play extended further than the temporal limits of the play itself. In other words, every moment of the play is part of a context of meanings derived from the action of the play already experienced and action yet to be experienced. But the action of the play is *experienceable* because the viewer possesses habits at least minimally relevant to the perception of the play. The action of the play and the viewer's experience of it cannot become aspects of a "single tension" unless the viewer possesses habits which can respond to the solicitation of the play and in turn answer with their own solicitation. Similarly, this concretion of self and world will not occur unless the energies of the play are so organized that they effect a dramatic reorganization of a major part of the field of habitual meanings.

Dewey conceived of consciousness as "that phase of a system of meanings which at a given time is undergoing re-direction, transitive transformation."[38] When consciousness is so conceived, Dewey's assertion that "every case of consciousness is dramatic" can be better understood with respect to habit. The relationship of the texts (ideas) of consciousness to the context of habitual meanings is intrinsically dramatic. Because text and context are not discrete elements but instead are joined by a "contextual field," the re-direction and reconstruction of meanings which characterizes the text of consciousness is organically related to the reconstruction and reorganization of the context of habitual meanings. Once certain meanings become discriminated as ideas or texts of consciousness, they do not become self-contained and isolated from the context of habitual meanings. Text and context exert a reciprocal influence upon each other, and hence what appears focally in consciousness is always characterized by some degree of drama since it is capable of further specification and elaboration through the influence of contextual meanings.

---

[38]*Experience and Nature,* 2nd ed., p. 251.

Dewey realized that those habitual meanings which constitute a contextual background cannot themselves be objects of consciousness while they are serving as context. Thus, Dewey was opposed to any theory of experience which emphasized its "surface" aspects. He says that

> experience is no stream, even though the stream of feelings and ideas that flow upon its surface is the part which philosophers love to traverse. Experience includes the enduring banks of natural constitution and acquired habit as well as the stream.[39]

Dewey is not merely saying that the "surface" of experience has a "depth" which cannot and should not be ignored. By comparing habits to the banks of a stream, Dewey is really saying that it is because the organism possesses structures in the form of habits that experience is capable of having a surface *and* a depth. If a stream did not have adequate banks, neither surface or depth could exist since there simply would be no stream. Similarly, unless the organism possessed certain persistent structures, there would be no possibility for it to have either surface or depth since it would lack any sort of temporal continuity. For this reason, Dewey says that "mind is, so to speak, structural, substantial, a constant background and foreground; perceptive consciousness is process, a series of heres and nows."[40]

According to Dewey: "The greater part of mind is only implicit in any conscious act or state; the field of mind—of operative meanings— is enormously wider than that of consciousness."[41] He says that

> if we consider the entire field from bright focus through the fore-conscious, the "fringe," to what is dim, sub-conscious "feeling," the focus corresponds to the point of imminent need, of urgency, the "fringe" corresponds to things that just have been reacted to or that will soon require to be looked after, while the remote outlying field corresponds to what does not have to be modified, and which may be dependably counted upon in dealing with imminent need.[42]

---

[39]*Experience and Nature,* 1st ed., p. 8.
[40]*Experience and Nature,* 2nd ed., p. 247.
[41]*Ibid.*
[42]*Ibid.,* pp. 253-54.

At first, this conception of the field of mind may seem rather schematic in view of Dewey's aversion to models and formulas which oversimplify the complexity and diversity of existence. Nevertheless, his specification of the field of mind into conscious, foreconscious, and subconscious, is merely a convenient way of outlining his more detailed discussion of the text-context relationship. Meanings which are "condensed at the focus of imminent redirection" constitute the text of consciousness. In becoming focal, these meanings have been directly influenced by, and have directly influenced, certain other meanings. Meanings which are non-focal but influence the character of the texts of consciousness constitute the context of that particular text. Obviously, certain contextual meanings will be more directly implicated in the character of the text than others. Hence, Dewey distinguishes between fringe and feeling or fore-conscious and sub-conscious in order to make provision for the fact that the entire field of habitual meanings never undergoes reconstruction or reorganization all at one time. Thus, although it is possible, and even necessary in aesthetic experience, that most of the "deepest" meanings of the sub-conscious may be directly and intensely involved in an aesthetic experience, they are all not reconstructed in that one experience. If *every* habitual meaning was reconstructed and reorganized into new configurations, there would be no basis for a continuous personal identity. "The sub-conscious of a civilized adult reflects all the habits he has acquired; that is to say, all the organic modifications he has undergone,"[43] and it is these sub-conscious habits which provide the taken for granted meanings necessary for the possession of a personal identity. Some, but not all, of these sub-conscious habits are reconstructed in an aesthetic experience.

This context of fore-conscious and sub-conscious habitual meanings makes possible what Dewey calls "*having* an experience." Without conscious deliberation, certain objects and events are immediately experienced *as* fearful, pleasurable, annoying, convincing, endless, hopeful, insistent, respectful, and so on. This context of habitual meanings is responsible for the way in which the object or event is immediately experienced *as*. Because the context of pre-objective (understood as including fore-conscious and sub-conscious meanings) habitual meanings is the source of the texts of consciousness, it is evident why Dewey con-

---

[43]*Ibid.*, p. 245.

sidered such terms as context, background, and fringe "too external" to
adequately describe how this system of taken for granted meanings
"suffuses, interpenetrates, colors" the texts of focal consciousness. Pre-
conscious habit is active, creative, and constitutive; it is the foundation
and source of thematic consciousness. Merleau-Ponty's summary of his
investigation into the habitual body could serve equally well as a summary of Dewey's work. Merleau-Ponty says: "We found beneath intentionality related to acts, or thetic intentionality, another kind which
is the condition of the former's possibility: namely an operative intentionality already at work before any positing or any judgment, a 'Logos
of the aesthetic world,' an 'art hidden in the depths of the human soul,'
one which like any art, is known only in its results."[44] The organic
structures which ground the human pole of intentionality are pre-conscious habits. When the role of pre-conscious habit in Dewey's philosophy of experience is properly understood, there is an added force
to his assertion that "experience is something quite other than 'consciousness,' that is, that which appears qualitatively and focally at a particular moment."[45] For both Dewey and Merleau-Ponty, man's sub-
jectivity—his identity as a "subject" or agent of action, as opposed to a
mere object—has its source in the dialectic he carries on with the
world through the operation of pre-reflective, pre-conscious habits.

When mind and consciousness are understood as aspects of a
"contextual field" of meanings, the nature of "intuition" and "imagination" appears to be less "mysterious" and "mystical" than it is commonly taken to be. An intuition is an immediately felt or 'had' meaning which has become, or is on the verge of becoming, a text of consciousness without being, so to speak, announced by a deliberate act
of thought. An intuition may provide one with a relatively determinate
meaning, in which case the meaning has been entirely formed and constituted by the operative intentionality of habit. In this case there is a
"quick and unexpected harmony" since there was no conscious anticipation of the appearance of a distinct meaning; the meaning moves from
context to text with such rapidity that there is no opportunity for any
positing of objects of conscious deliberation. An intuition may, however, require a certain amount of deliberate attention before it becomes

[44]*Phenomenology*, p. 429.
[45]*Experience and Nature*, 1st ed., p. 7.

a text. Unlike the first type of intuition, and intuition of this sort requires conscious effort on the part of the subject in order to achieve "the union of old and new, of foreground and background."[46] It is clear from his discussion that Dewey is talking about intuition in the sense of "intuitive insight," i.e., he is concerned with that sort of intuition which marks a movement of a meaning, either rapidly or slowly, from context to text. Dewey certainly was aware that there are different senses of intuition, but he was concerned with intuitive insight because it has a more direct connection with the text-context relationship.

As Dewey conceives of them, intuition and imagination are closely related; in the second chapter he even speaks of "imaginative intuitions."[47] Imagination, like intuition, has suffered at the hands of mystics, and Dewey notes that "more perhaps than any other phase of the human contribution, it has been treated as a special and self-contained faculty, different from others in possession of mysterious potencies."[48] Yet, this need not be the case if it is remembered that "concrete habits do all the perceiving, recognizing, imagining, recalling, judging, conceiving and reasoning that is done."[49] An imaginative experience is marked by an interpenetration of habitual meanings in response to a solicitation from some intentional object. In Dewey's words: "An imaginative experience is what happens when varied materials of sense quality, emotion, and meaning come together in a union that marks a new birth in the world."[50] The union or concretion of perceptual, emotional, and cognitive habits is the basis of an imaginative experience.

When imagination is seen to be a function of habit and not some sort of self-contained mysterious power, it can be understood why Dewey says that "it designates a quality that animates and pervades all processes of making and observation. It is a *way* of seeing and feeling things as they compose an integral whole."[51] To speak of a person as "lacking imagination," one is commenting about that person's habits —the kinds of habits he has and their relationship to each other. Thus, a person may have fairly complex, sophisticated habits such as those

---

[46]*Art as Experience*, p. 226.
[47]*Ibid.*, p. 34.
[48]*Ibid.*, p. 267.
[49]Dewey, *Human Nature*, p. 177.
[50]*Art as Experience*, p. 267.
[51]*Ibid.*

possessed by an architect. If, however, the architect's field of habitual meanings never becomes tensed to the point where there is a "welding together"[52] or concretion of these habitual meanings, his plans will be technically correct but not particularly inspired, i.e., lacking in any sort of imaginative vision. On the other hand, the habits of a grocery clerk may be relatively simple and uncomplicated, yet because his field of habitual meanings is tensed and thus available for a fusion or concretion of these meanings, his display of a new product may evidence more imagination than the work of the architect. The formal difference in imagination between the architect and the grocery clerk lies in the nature of their respective *fields* of habitual meanings and not in the complexity of the habits themselves. The ideal conditions of imagination are exhibited in the person whose habits are subtle, varied, and complex, and whose habits are constituents of a field marked by tension and thus readily available for fusion or concretion in an expressive act of saying, doing, or making.

Imagination is not, then, a "gift" reserved for "gifted" people. Whenever habitual self and world interact, and interact in such a manner that "the background of organized meanings" of the self is modified in some way, then there is some degree of expression and imagination. The interaction of habitual self and world is an adventure, for Dewey says that "there is always some measure of adventure in the meeting of mind and universe, and this adventure is, in its measure, imagination."[53] Dewey is saying here that the interaction or dialectic of self and world is dramatic, and since imagination is a function of the dramatic accommodation of self to world and world to self, "imagination is primarily dramatic rather than lyric, whether it takes the form of the play enacted on the stage, of the told story or silent soliloquy."[54]

An imaginative experience is a fusion or concretion of contextual, habitual meanings, and the meanings or texts of the present circumstances. In an aesthetic experience, the drama of habit is celebrated through an intensification and purification of its pre-objective intentionality. There is an intensified concretion of past, present, and future meanings. In addition, the field of pre-reflective, pre-conscious habitual meanings becomes tensed and readily available for reconstruction and reor-

[52]*Ibid.*
[53]*Ibid.*
[54]*Experience and Nature*, 2nd ed., p. 76.

ganization. As a result of this intensification of the intentionality of habit, the mutual, reciprocal implication of self and world is accentuated and intensified. Imagination is based upon the drama of habit; imagination itself *is* the drama of habit made conscious. So, far from being a transcendence of the supposed limitations of habit, imagination is a testimony to the world-founding powers and possibilities of habit. Merleau-Ponty says that "what is acquired is truly acquired only if it is taken up again in a fresh momentum of thought."[55] Habit is the basis of such momentum, and imagination its vehicle and realization.

---

[55]*Phenomenology,* p. 130,

CHAPTER VII

THE HABIT OF MEANING

Merleau-Ponty says that "we are not asking the logician to take into consideration experiences which, in the light of reason, are non-sensical or contradictory, we merely want to push back the boundaries of what makes sense for us, and reset the narrow zone of thematic significance within that of non-thematic significance which embraces it."[1] This is a fair summary of both Dewey's and Merleau-Ponty's position that man is a sense-giving being on a non-thematic or pre-reflective, pre-conscious level of experience. Sense-giving, or sense-making, is an intentional activity implicating self and world in a "single tension." In an aesthetic experience, this "single tension" or concretion of self and world is accentuated and intensified.

Dewey's *Art as Experience* is more than a study in aesthetics. It is a study in the pre-objective intentionality of habit. In view of the fact that habit is commonly neglected when the general features of Dewey's philosophy are discussed, it is not surprising that its role in aesthetic experience has been completely overlooked. Nevertheless, it is perfectly obvious that the pre-objective intentionality of habit pervades *Art as Experience* starting with Dewey's discussion of the "immediate thought" of the savage, and ending with his recognition that industrial surroundings are affecting "the habits of the eye." Dewey himself is partly to blame for the neglect which has been shown to the pre-objective intentionality of habit as it functions in *Art as Experience*. It seems almost as if Dewey made a conscious effort to avoid using the word "habit" in his discussion, and instead substituted "attitude," "disposition," "interest," "organic modification," "self," and "mind." All these terms, however, Dewey took to be variant ways of referring to the functioning of habit, the concept which he chose to be the basis of his philosophy of experience and experienced meaning.

In a certain sense, the pre-objective intentionality of habit is the

---

[1]*Ibid.*, p. 275.

most basic context of Dewey's book. It is so pervasively present that Dewey himself takes it almost too much for granted. There is no line of thought in *Art as Experience* which escapes the influence of Dewey's understanding of habit's pre-objective intentionality. Ironically, by virtue of its pervasive presence, it is likely to be unperceived and thus unappreciated. By using Merleau-Ponty's work on the pre-objective intentionality of the habitual body as a means of gaining some perspective on Dewey, what is context in *Art as Experience* can be brought into sharper focus.

When this focusing is effected, it becomes apparent that Dewey's effort to "push back the boundaries of what makes sense for us," was at the very heart of his philosophical effort. Rarely has a philosopher with Dewey's profound respect for science affirmed so consistently that "the world which is lived, suffered and enjoyed as well as logically thought of, has the last word in all human inquiries and surmises."[2] Dewey shared with Merleau-Ponty a desire to recover what the latter referred to as "the prescientific life of consciousness which alone endows scientific operations with meaning and to which these latter always refer back."[3] Dewey, no less than Husserl or Merleau-Ponty, recognized that predicative judgment could not be separated from that pre-reflective, habitual ordering of the world which prepares and ultimately fulfills the human possibilities of reflection and judgment.

A recognition of Dewey's belief that "the visible is set in the invisible,"[4] the known in the lived, entails a major reassessment of his epistemology, particularly his presumed fascination with scientific method. Dewey never weakened in his conviction that "knowledge is instrumental to the enrichment of immediate experience through the control over action that it exercises."[5] This statement, and the many others like it, were not merely verbalisms designed to soften Dewey's image as a celebrant of science and its application to all areas of human experience. Dewey's belief that "knowledge itself must be experienced; it must be had,"[6] evidences his understanding that even the most dazzling achievements of thought are grounded in the pre-objective being of habit.

[2]*Experience and Nature,* 1st ed., p. 12.
[3]*Phenomenology,* pp. 58-59.
[4]*Experience and Nature,* 2nd ed., p. 40.
[5]*Art as Experience,* p. 290.
[6]*Experience and Nature,* 1st ed., p. 31.

Part of the genius of Dewey was that despite his enormous respect for scientific and reflective method, he never fell victim to what Merleau-Ponty called the "mistake of reflective philosophies," the tendency "to believe that the thinking subject can absorb into its thinking or appropriate without remainder the object of its thought, that our being can be brought down to our knowledge."[7] Few contemporary philosophers have equaled the quality of Dewey's insistence that reflection is our most reliable method for securing meaning. "The striving," he says, "to make stability of meaning prevail over the instability of events is the main task of intelligent human effort."[8] Fewer philosophers, though, have matched Dewey's awareness that the lucidity of meanings stabilized in reflection are not fixed accomplishments. Reflected meanings sedimented in habit are not, Merleau-Ponty says, "a final gain, they continually draw their sustenance from my present thought, they offer me a meaning, but I give it back to them."[9] The visible is indeed set in the invisible: their reciprocal influence in aesthetic experience is an intensification of the ambiguity and fragility of the habit of meaning.

When *Art as Experience* is viewed as one of Dewey's most profound treatments of his ontology of sense, it becomes clear that his notion of habit is not merely an isolated feature of his social psychology, as it is sometimes supposed. It is the critical center of Dewey's philosophy of experience, of which *Art as Experience* and *Experience and Nature* are the most systematic statements. When the pre-objective intentionality of habit is recognized and understood, it then may be possible to appreciate the implications contained in Dewey's affirmation that "through habits formed in intercourse with the world, we also inhabit the world." Certainly, such a statement offers at least as much of a challenge to philosophy as Merleau-Ponty's conviction that "habit expresses our power of dilating our being in the world."

---

[7]*Phenomenology*, p. 62.
[8]*Experience and Nature*, 2nd ed., p. 45.
[9]*Phenomenology*, p. 130.

SELECTED BIBLIOGRAPHY

DEWEY
  BOOKS

Dewey, John. *The Influence of Darwin on Philosophy: And Other Essays in Contemporary Thought*. Bloomington: Indiana University Press, 1910.
——. *Democracy and Education: An Introduction to the Philosophy of Education*. New York: Macmillan Company, 1916.
——. *Essays in Experimental Logic*. New York: Dover Publications, Inc., 1916.
——. *Human Nature and Conduct: An Introduction to Social Psychology*. New York: Modern Library, 1922.
——. *Experience and Nature*. Chicago: Open Court Publishing Company, 1925.
——. *The Public and Its Problems*. Chicago: Swallow Press, Inc., 1927.
——. *Experience and Nature*. 2nd ed. Illinois: Open Court Publishing Company, 1929.
——. *The Quest for Certainty: A Study of the Relation of Knowledge and Action*. New York: Minton, Balch & Company, 1929.
——. *Philosophy and Civilization*. New York: Minton, Balch & Company, 1931.
——. *How We Think: A Restatement of the Relation of Reflective Thinking to the Educative Process*. Boston: D.C. Heath and Company, 1933.
——. *Art as Experience*. New York: Minton, Balch & Company, 1934.
——. *Experience and Education*. New York: Collier Books, 1938.
——. *Logic: The Theory of Inquiry*. New York: Holt, Rinehart and Winston, 1938.
——, and Bentley, Arthur F. *Knowing and the Known*. Boston: Beacon Press, 1949.

EDITED COLLECTIONS OF ARTICLES AND ESSAYS

Dewey, John. *John Dewey on Experience, Nature, and Freedom.* ed. by
    Richard J. Bernstein. New York: Liberal Arts Press, 1960.
————. *John Dewey: Philosophy, Psychology and Social Practice.*
    ed. by Joseph Ratner. New York: Capricorn Books, 1963.
————. *The Philosophy of John Dewey: The Structure of Experi-
    ence,* Vol. I; *The Philosophy of John Dewey: The Lived Ex-
    perience,* Vol. II. ed. by John J. McDermott. New York: G. P.
    Putman's Sons, 1973.

ARTICLES

Dewey, John. "Immediate Empiricism." *The Journal of Philosophy,* II
    (October 26, 1905), 597-99.
————. "The Knowledge Experience and Its Relationships." *The
    Journal of Philosophy, II* (November 23, 1905), 652-57.
————. "The Knowledge Experience Again." *The Journal of Phi-
    losophy,* II (December 21, 1905), 707-11.
————. "Reality as Experience." *The Journal of Philosophy,* III
    (May 10, 1906), 253-57.
————. "Pure Experience and Reality: A Disclaimer." *Philosophical
    Review,* XVI (July, 1907), 419-22.
————. "Meaning and Existence." *The Journal of Philosophy,* XXV
    (June 21, 1928), 345-53.
————. "Inquiry and Indeterminateness of Situation." *The Journal
    of Philosophy,* XXXIX (May 21, 1942), 290-96.
————. "Experience and Existence: A Comment." *Philosophy and
    Phenomenological Research,* IX (June, 1949), 709-13.

BOOKS ON DEWEY

Bernstein, Richard J. *John Dewey.* New York: Washington Square
    Press, Inc., 1966.
Dykhuizen, George. *The Life and Mind of John Dewey.* Carbondale:
    Southern Illinois University Press, 1973.
Geiger, George R. *John Dewey in Perspective: A Reassessment.* New
    York: McGraw-Hill Book Company, 1958.
Gouinlock, James. *John Dewey's Philosophy of Value.* New York: Hu-
    manities Press, 1972.

ARTICLES ON DEWEY

Ames, Van Meter. "John Dewey as Aesthetician." *The Journal of Aesthetics and Art Criticism,* XII (December, 1953), 145-68.

Bakewell, Charles M. "An Open Letter to Professor Dewey Concerning Immediate Empiricism." *The Journal of Philosophy,* II (September 14, 1905), 520-22.

Bernstein, Richard J. "Dewey's Naturalism." *The Review of Metaphysics,* XIII (December, 1959), 340-53.

————. "John Dewey's Metaphysics of Experience." *The Journal of Philosophy,* LVIII (January 5, 1961), 5-14.

Bode, B. H. "Cognitive Experience and Its Objects." *The Journal of Philosophy,* II (November 23, 1905), 658-63.

Eames, S. Morris. "Primary Experience in the Philosophy of John Dewey." *The Monist,* XLVIII (July, 1964), 407-18.

Kahn, Sholom J. "Experience and Existence in Dewey's Naturalistic Metaphysics." *Philosophy and Phenomenological Research,* IX (December, 1948), 316-21.

Kennedy, Gail. "Dewey's Concept of Experience: Determinate, Indeterminate, and Problematic." *The Journal of Philosophy,* LVI (October 8, 1959), 801-814.

————. "Comment on Professor Bernstein's Paper: 'John Dewey's Metaphysics of Experience.' " *The Journal of Philosophy,* LVIII (January 5, 1961), 14-21.

Leighton, J. A. "Cognitive Thought and 'Immediate Empiricism.' " *The Journal of Philosophy,* III (March 29, 1906), 174-180.

Mackay, D. S. "What Does Mr. Dewey Mean By an 'Indeterminate Situation'?" *The Journal of Philosophy,* XXXIX (March 12, 1942), 141-48.

Pepper, Stephen C. "The Concept of Fusion in Dewey's Aesthetic Theory." *The Journal of Aesthetics and Art Criticism,* XII (December, 1953), 169-176.

Smith, John E. "John Dewey: Philosopher of Experience." *The Review of Metaphysics,* XIII (September, 1959), 60-78.

Welsh, Paul. "Some Metaphysical Assumptions in Dewey's Philosophy." *The Journal of Philosophy,* LI (December 23, 1954), 861-867,

Wienpahl, Paul D. "Dewey's Theory of Language and Meaning," in *John Dewey: Philosopher of Science and Freedom,* ed. by Sidney Hook. New York: The Dial Press, 1950.

Woodbridge, Frederick J. E. "Of What Sort Is Cognitive Experience?" *The Journal of Philosophy,* II (October 12, 1905), 573-576.

Zink, Sidney. "The Concept of Continuity in Dewey's Theory of Es-
thetics." *The Philosophical Review,* LII (July, 1943), 392-400.

MERLEAU-PONTY
BOOKS

Merleau-Ponty, Maurice. *The Structure of Behavior.* trans. by Alden
L. Fisher. Boston: Beacon Press, 1942.
————. *Phenomenology of Perception.* trans. by Colin Smith. New
York: Humanities Press, 1962.
————. *The Visible and the Invisible.* trans. by Alphonso Lingis.
Evanston: Northwestern University Press, 1968.

BOOKS ON MERLEAU-PONTY

Bannan, John F. *The Philosophy of Merleau-Ponty.* New York: Har-
court, Brace & World, Inc., 1967.
Barral, Mary Rose. *Merleau-Ponty: The Role of the Body-Subject in
Interpersonal Relations.* Pittsburgh: Duquesne University Press,
1965.
Gillan, Garth., ed. *The Horizons of the Flesh: Critical Perspectives on
the Thought of Merleau-Ponty.* Carbondale: Southern Illinois
University Press, 1973.
Kaelin, Eugene F. *An Existentialist Aesthetic: The Theories of Sartre
and Merleau-Ponty.* Madison: University of Wisconsin Press,
1962.
Kwant, Remy C. *The Phenomenological Philosophy of Merleau-Ponty.*
Pittsburgh: Duquesne University Press, 1963.
Langan, Thomas. *Merleau-Ponty's Critique of Reason.* New Haven:
Yale University Press, 1966.
Rabil, Albert, Jr. *Merleau-Ponty: Existentialist of the Social World.*
New York: Columbia University Press, 1967.

ARTICLES AND ESSAYS ON MERLEAU-PONTY

Ballard, Edward G. "The Philosophy of Merleau-Ponty." *Tulane Studies
in Philosophy,* IX (1960), 165-87.
————. "On Cognition of the Precognitive—Merleau-Ponty." *Philosophical Quarterly,* II (July, 1961), 238-44.

Bannan, John F. "Philosophical Reflection and the Phenomenology of Merleau-Ponty." *The Review of Metaphysics,* VIII (March, 1955), 418-42.

Dillon, M. C. "Gestalt Theory and Merleau-Ponty's Concept of Intentionality." *Man and World,* IV (Nov., 1971), pp. 436-459.

Dreyfus, Hubert L., and Todes, S. J. "The Three Worlds of Merleau-Ponty." *Philosophy and Phenomenological Research.* XXII (June, 1962), 559-65.

Gerber, Rudolph J. "Merleau-Ponty: The Dialectic of Consciousness and World." *Man and World, II* (February, 1969), 83-107.

Kullman, Michael, and Taylor, Charles. "The Pre-Objective World." *The Review of Metaphysics,* XII (September, 1958), 108-32.

Langan, Thomas. "Maurice Merleau-Ponty: In Memoriam." *Philosophy and Phenomenological Research,* XXIII (December, 1962), 205-16.

Scharfstein, Ben-Ami. "Bergson and Merleau-Ponty: A Preliminary Comparison." *The Journal of Philosophy,* LII (July 7, 1955), 380-86.

Schmitt, Richard. "Maurice Merleau-Ponty." *The Review of Metaphysics,* XIX (March, 1966; June, 1966), 493-516, 728-41.

Smith, Colin. "The Notion of Object in the Phenomenology of Merleau-Ponty." *Philosophy,* XXXIX (April, 1964), 110-19.

Spiegelberg, Herbert. "The Phenomenological Philosophy of Maurice Merleau-Ponty." in *The Phenomenological Movement: A Historical Introduction,* Vol. II. The Hague: Martinus Nijhoff, 1965, pp. 516-62.

GENERAL
BOOKS

Bouman, Jan C. *The Figure-Ground Phenomenon in Experimental and Phenomenological Psychology.* Stockholm: Fallmarks Boktryckeri, 1968.

Buchler, Justus. *Toward a General Theory of Human Judgment.* New York: Columbia University Press, 1951.

————. *Nature and Judgment.* New York: Columbia University Press, 1955.

Dufrenne, Mikel. *The Phenomenology of Aesthetic Experience.* trans. by Edward S. Casey, et. al. Evanston: Northwestern University Press, 1973.

Edie, James M., ed. *An Invitation to Phenomenology: Studies in the Philosophy of Experience.* Chicago: Quadrangle Books, 1965.

————., ed. *Phenomenology in America: Studies in the Philosophy of Experience.* Chicago: Quadrangle Books, 1967.

————., ed. *New Essays in Phenomenology: Studies in the Philosophy of Experience.* Chicago: Quadrangle Books, 1969.

Fingarette, Herbert. *The Self in Transformation: Psychoanalysis, Philosophy, and the Life of the Spirit.* New York: Harper Torchbooks, 1963.

Garfinkel, Harold. *Studies in Ethnomethodology.* New York: Prentice-Hall, Inc., 1967.

Gendlin, Eugene T. *Experiencing and the Creation of Meaning: A Philosophical and Psychological Approach to the Subjective.* New York: Free Press of Glencoe, 1962.

Gurwitsch, Aron. *The Field of Consciousness.* Pittsburgh: Duquesne University Press, 1964.

Husserl, Edmund. *Cartesian Meditations: An Introduction to Phenomenology.* trans. by Dorion Cairns. The Hague: Martinus Nijhoff, 1960.

————. *Experience and Judgment: Investigations in a Genealogy of Logic.* trans. by James S. Churchill and Karl Ameriks. Evanston: Northwestern University Press, 1973.

James, William. *The Principles of Psychology,* 2 vols. New York: Dover Publications, Inc., 1890.

Kockelmans, Joseph J., ed. *Phenomenology: The Philosophy of Edmund Husserl and Its Interpretation.* New York: Anchor Books, 1967.

Kuhn, Thomas S. *The Structure of Scientific Revolutions.* Chicago: University of Chicago Press, 1970.

Kwant, Remy C. *Phenomenology of Expression.* Pittsburgh: Duquesne University Press, 1969.

Mack, Robert D. *The Appeal to Immediate Experience: Philosophic Method in Bradley, Whitehead, and Dewey.* New York: Books for Libraries Press, 1945.

Mathur, D. C. *Naturalistic Philosophies of Experience: Studies in James, Dewey and Farber Against the Background of Husserl's Phenomenology.* Missouri: Warren H. Green, Inc., 1971.

Randall, John Herman, Jr. *Nature and Historical Experience: Essays in Naturalism and in the Theory of History.* New York: Columbia University Press, 1958.

Ricoeur, Paul. *Freedom and Nature: The Voluntary and the Involuntary.* trans. by Erazim V. Kohák. Evanston: Northwestern University Press, 1966.

Scheffler, Israel. *Four Pragmatists: A Critical Introduction to Peirce, James, Mead, and Dewey.* New York: Humanities Press, 1974.

Schrag, Calvin O. *Experience and Being: Prolegomena to a Future Ontology,* Evanston, Ill.: Northwestern University Press, 1969.

Schutz, Alfred. *Reflections on the Problem of Relevance.* New Haven: Yale University Press, 1970.

Sheridan, James F. Jr. *Once More From the Middle: A Philosophical Anthropology.* Athens: Ohio University Press, 1973.

Smith, Colin. *Contemporary French Philosophy: A Study in Norms and Values.* New York: Barnes and Noble Inc., 1964.

Thevenaz, Pierre. *What is Phenomenology?* Chicago: Quadrangle Books, 1962.

Ushenko, Andrew Paul. *The Field Theory of Meaning.* Ann Arbor: University of Michigan Press, 1958.

Weisman, Avery D. *The Existential Core of Psychoanalysis: Reality Sense and Responsibility.* Boston: Little, Brown and Company, 1965.

Wild, John. *The Challenge of Existentialism.* Bloomington: Indiana University Press, 1955.

————. *Existence and the World of Freedom.* New Jersey: Prentice-Hall, Inc., 1963.

————. *The Radical Empiricism of William James.* New York: Anchor Books, 1970.

Wilshire, Bruce. *William James and Phenomenology: A Study of "The Principles of Psychology."* Bloomington: Indiana University Press, 1968.

————. *Metaphysics: An Introduction to Philosophy.* New York: Pegasus, 1969.

Yolton, John W. *Thinking and Perceiving: A Study in the Philosophy of Mind.* Illinois: Open Court Publishing Company, 1962.

ARTICLES AND ESSAYS

Carr, David. "Husserl's Problematic Concept of the Life-World." *American Philosophical Quarterly,* VII (Oct., 1970), pp. 331-39.

Corello, Anthony V. "Some Structural Parallels in Phenomenology and Pragmatism," in *Life-World and Consciousness: Essays for Aron Gurwitsch*, ed. by Lester E. Embree. Evanston: Northwestern University Press, 1972.

Edie, James M. Expression and Metaphor." *Philosophy and Phenomenological Research*. XXIII (June, 1963), 538-61.

Harrison, Ross. "The Concept of Prepredicative Experience," in *Phenomenology and Philosophical Understanding*, ed. by Edo Pivčević. New York: Cambridge University Press, 1975.

Lingis, Alphonso. "The Elemental Background," in *New Essays in Phenomenology: Studies in the Philosophy of Experience*, ed. by James M. Edie. Chicago: Quadrangle Books, 1969.

O'Malley, John B. "Seeing—Meaning—Making." *The Human Context*, II (Spring, 1970), pp. 48-68.

Rosenthal, Sandra B. "Recent Perspectives on American Pragmatism." *Transactions of the Charles S. Peirce Society*, X (Spring, 1974; Summer, 1974), pp. 76-93, 166-84.

Silber, John R. "Being and Doing: A Study of Status Responsibility and Voluntary Responsibility," in *Phenomenology in America: Studies in the Philosophy of Experience*, ed. by James M. Edie. Chicago: Quadrangle Books, 1967.

Spiegelberg, Herbert. "Toward a Phenomenology of Experience." *American Philosophical Quarterly*, I (October, 1964), 325-32.

Wild, John. "Contemporary Phenomenology and the Problem of Existence." *Philosophy and Phenomenological Research*, XX (December, 1959), 166-80.

Yolton, John W. "The Form and Development of Experience." *Acta Psychologica*, XXI (1963), 357-70.

————. "Perceptual Consciousness." *Knowledge and Necessity*. Royal Institute of Philosophy Lectures, Vol. III, 1968-69. New York: St. Martin's Press, Inc., 1970, 34-50.